# Through a Glass Darkly:
# A Crisis Considered

# Through a Glass Darkly:
# A Crisis Considered

*Edited by Michael Watts*

*Gracewing.*

Fowler Wright Books
Leominster Herefordshire

First Published 1993
Gracewing
Fowler Wright Books
2 Southern Avenue, Leominster
Herefordshire HR6 0QF

## Gracewing Books are distributed

In New Zealand by
Catholic Supplies Ltd
80 Adelaide Rd
Wellington
New Zealand

In Australia by
Charles Paine Pty
8 Ferris Street
North Parramatta
NSW 2151 Australia

In USA by
Morehouse Publishing
PO Box 1321
Harrisburg
PA17105

ISBN 0 85244 240 8

Typesetting by Print Origination (NW) Limited Formby, Liverpool L37 8EG
Printed and bound by The Cromwell Press, Broughton Gifford, Melksham

# Contents

# Appendices:

# ADMG

This volume is dedicated to the memory of:

Miss Margaret Clarabut

Miss Evelyn Light

Benefactresses of

The Society for the Maintenance of the Faith

*Requiescant in Pace*

# Editor's Note

I wish to place on record my warm appreciation of the ready way in which the contributors responded to my request that they would make time in already busy lives to write these essays, and of the assistance given equally readily by Christine Simmonds in the preparation of the manuscript and by Tom Longford, without whose vigilance, practical assistance and encouragement this book would not have been published.

Michael Watts
Secretary
The Society for the Maintenance of the Faith

# Acknowledgements

Acknowledgements and thanks are given to *The Church Times, The Month* and *The Catholic Herald* for permission to quote from their pages; S.P.C.K for permission to use extracts from *Doctrine in the Church of England* and *Report of the Archbishops' Commission on Ecclesiastical Courts*; the Coronation Oath and extracts from *The Book of Common Prayer,* the rights in which are invested in the Crown, are reproduced by permission of the Crown's Patentee, Cambridge University Press; to the Central Board of Finance of the Church of England and Church House Publishing for the extracts from the *Proceedings of the General Synod, Canons of the Church of England, Episcopal Ministry, The Priesthood of the Ordained Ministry, The Ordination of Women to the Priesthood* and *The Manchester Statement*; to Mowbray for the extract from Adrian Hasting's *Robert Runcie*; to Darton, Longman & Todd for the extracts from *God Alive* and Rahner's *Theological Investigations*; to the Church Literature Association for the extract from *Saepius Officio*; to Penguin Books Ltd for the extract from *Bede's History of the English Church and People*; to Church House Publishing for the extract from *ARCIC II*; to Paulist Press, U.S.A., for the extract from H. Meyer's and L. Fischer's *Growth in Agreement: Reports and Agreed Statements of Ecumenical Conversations on a World Level*; to S.P.C.K. for permission to use an extract from their book *Ecumenical Theology*; to S.P.C.K. for permission to use extracts from *Anglicanism: The Thought and Practice of the Church of*

*England from the Religious Literature of the Seventeenth Century*; to J. Kent and R. Murray (eds) for permission to use an extract from *Church Membership and Intercommunion*. The publishers also acknowledge the use of material from Dom Anselm Hughes's *Rivers of the Flood*; K. E. Kirk *Beauty and Bands*.

Also acknowledgements and thanks are given to the Bishop of Chichester for permission to use an extract from his Address to the Federation of Catholic Priests.

All efforts have been made to check the copyright of all material quoted. Despite extensive searching a few could not be traced, and will be acknowledged if possible in any future editions.

# Preface

I am very happy to commend this important book. In the General Synod debate of November 11th there was very little meeting of minds. The supporters of the legislation spoke almost entirely about the ordination of women in itself. The opponents mostly about the questions of authority and ecclesiology raised by it. Since the vote it has become apparent that many more people are concerned about its implications for the Catholicity, Authority and Unity of the Church than was obvious last year. These underlying issues have emerged more clearly from the confusing mists of secular/ecclesial feminism which have obscured them and to a certain extent still do so, at a popular level, and seriously damage the wider question of the ministry of women in the Church.

These essays have been written not in a spirit of polemic, but to assist lay people in particular to understand the complex issues which have been raised by the decision. Quite deliberately the substansive issue, whether or not it can ever be right to ordain a woman to the priesthood has not been addressed. Among the contributors there is such a variety of view point about that matter as can be found in a large number of parishes throughout the country.

Of necessity the book has to be wide-ranging in its concerns. Specialists in Sacramental Theology, the history of the Church of England, its Authority, its Canon Law and other aspects of its life have contributed essays dealing with the implications of the Synod's decision from their particular expertise.

I hope that it will be welcomed as a stimulus to the debate about these issues which will continue for the foreseeable future.

May it help all those who are concerned for the unity and peace of the Church of England at this time.

+ Eric Cicestr:
The Rt Revd Eric Kemp, Bishop of Chichester

Easter 1993

# I

# A Voice from the Pew

## *Margaret Laird*

Bishop William Stubbs claimed that 'a brief reflection' [1] solved the particular mystery which confronted him. However, it is unlikely that even the prolonged period of reflection afforded to the Church of England, while Parliament debates the legislation for the ordination of women, will provide a satisfactory solution to what many laypeople consider a great mystery, the divisiveness which has resulted from the General Synod's decision.

There is no doubt that the people in the pew face challenging years ahead and, if some vestige of unity is to be maintained in the Church of England, it is essential to identify their difficulties and to ensure that they have a clear understanding of the issues at stake.

During the period when the ordination of women was being discussed at parochial and deanery levels, laypeople encountered many problems. They were never quite clear whether they were meant to be considering the principle behind the legislation or the legislation itself. Furthermore, the arguments put forward by the opponents did not seem to relate to those of the proponents and, as both sides substantiated their claims with support from the Scriptures, many, like one speaker[2] in the General Synod, honestly did not know which way to vote. "I have not been given the wisdom," he said.

*1*

For many people in the pew, the decision eventually made by the General Synod seemed a matter of common sense. Arguments based on a "leap of faith" and "the Spirit of the age" can be very persuasive. Others in our congregations felt, and still feel, instinctively opposed to the prospect of women priests but so often they lacked the specialist knowledge which appeared to be necessary to support their case. What, however, the majority of the people in the pew did not realize (largely because it had not been spelt out in the preliminary discussions) was that the acceptance of the first clause of the legislation, which seemed straightforward enough, has undermined two fundamental principles of Anglicanism. No longer will members of the Church of England be able to claim that they are required to receive nothing as of faith save that which is upheld by Scripture and the tradition of the early Church, nor that they have and are held together by a commonly accepted ministry. These are just two of the issues, amongst others, which will be developed in the essays which follow.

The long drawn out and continuing controversy has tended to cloud rather than clarify the situation. For example, the conclusion to which one was led after studying the Bishops' Report of 1988 was strangely reminiscent of that reached after reading the Book of Job, that there really was no clear cut answer. Then, after the vote, the statement[3] by the House of Bishops in the following January led to further complications. In this, the Bishops gave their assurance that, although the Synodical decision had been made in favour of the legislation, those who continued to oppose it would be recognized as "valued and loyal Anglicans", pastoral provision would be made for them and even ordinands who opposed the ordination of women might still be accepted. If the matter were still so unclear, many laypeople have asked whether it would not have been wiser to have postponed the vote until the theological and ecclesiological questions which seem to have been highlighted by the decision itself, had been probed more deeply.

In the early stages of the controversy, the people in the pew found it difficult to disassociate their thinking on this issue from trends in the Church and in society which were favourable to an affirmative vote. There has, for example, been a new emphasis within the Church on the work of the Holy Spirit. For congregations greatly influenced by the 'Renewal' or charismatic movements, the idea that the Holy Spirit, who leads us into "all truth"[4], might be revealing a new truth, was an exciting challenge. The Holy Spirit's guidance of the Church over the decision to baptise Gentiles was quoted as a precedent. References, however, to the Holy Spirit as the preserver of continuity, "the Counsellor, who will bring to your remembrance all that I have said to you,"[5] enabling Christians to recall and proclaim the basic Gospel message, to protect the traditions of the Church and the fundamental truths of the faith did not have such a wide appeal to those who wished to see "all things new". Yet, in his account of that much quoted Council of Jerusalem, the writer of the Acts of the Apostles implied that it was the Holy Spirit who inspired James, the brother of the Lord, to remember the words of the prophet Amos[6], thus showing that God's purpose for the Gentiles was already inherent in the prophetic tradition and not the revelation of a new truth. When this same Biblical passage could be used to support both sides of the argument, how could people in the pew discern what the Spirit was saying to the Church of England about the ordination of women? Some influential Church leaders, however, proclaimed their own firmly held conviction that to vote against women priests would be to resist the guidance of the Holy Spirit. Many laypeople, even those with reservations, somewhat disturbed by such a claim, eventually, when faced with the actual legislation, voted in favour of it.

It was evident from parochial and deanery discussions that there was a suspicion on the part of many people in the pew that the movement for the ordination of women was a passing fashion fostered by secular feminism. Many of their doubts, however, were dispelled by feminist theologians who, with their selective use of the Biblical text and skilful interpretations of Scripture, managed to convince people that Jesus would have been on their side. That this would have been the case was rarely questioned although it must be said that many modern scholars place Jesus well within the mainstream of First Century Judaism, suggesting that his teaching was distinctive but not particularly revolutionary. Certainly, he was remarkably free in his attitude to women but he was not the inaugurator of a new social order in which primary responsibility in the home no longer rested with the mother. He aimed at equal consideration for all but not at undermining a generally accepted feature of the human condition, that men and women have equal but distinctive rôles, an understanding which Christians have traditionally seen in the Genesis doctrine of creation.

Such reasoning, however, did not attract wide support in that it conflicted with the most secular and most persuasive of all the arguments used by the proponents, the plea for 'equal rights'. As today's women have assumed a new status and desire equality in all the professions, should they not also be given equal rights and opportunities in the Church? That the Church might be called to restore the balance to a society which Von Balthasar described as "motherless and fatherless" and that she often witnesses more effectively by swimming against the secular tide, was not an acceptable idea to those anxious to adapt the faith to meet the modern world and to mould the Church into a more fashionable shape and form. Yet, as Dr Graham Leonard once commented, "The irony is that, though men reject the Church when she is true to herself, they despise her when she is conformed to the world."[7]

Another difficulty for the people in the pew was that most of them could play only a limited rôle in these early discussions, for they lacked, through no fault of their own, the theological background which was necessary to challenge some of the arguments put forward by the proponents. To respond to the pleas for "natural justice" so that women deacons, as well as men, could test their vocations to the priesthood, made sense. The more obscure stance of the opponents, who claimed that Divine and human justice cannot always be equated, and explained that what appears unjust or unfair by worldly standards is not necessarily evil but could be part of God's plan, for

"God's ways are not our ways," was more difficult. It was, however, Biblical in origin but not so much in tune with Twentieth Century thought.

Frequently the proponents claimed that, if the incarnation had taken place in the Twentieth Century, Jesus would have chosen both male and female disciples as the Apostles, and this too required a theological response. In both the Old Testament and the New Testament, it is made clear that God in his sovereignty can act as he chooses, when he chooses and through whomsoever he chooses. This "election theology", not perhaps altogether familiar to many people in the pew, is summarized in Romans 9-11. So the opponents claimed, if God chose to reveal himself through his son (not a daughter) in the 'fullness of time', at a time when it was not acceptable to have female Apostles, it was surely an act of divine *significance* and not of divine *oversight*.

When faced by the legislation itself, laypeople soon found that even more questions began to arise. Did the Synod of the Church of England have the authority to take this decision? It soon became clear that to consider such questions it was necessary to have some knowledge of Church history. Historians themselves differed widely in their interpretation of the Reformation and in their definitions of the Church of England, and most laypeople, without specialist knowledge, were totally dependent on the interpretation they were given. That the church was both Catholic and Reformed was generally accepted, but what exactly did this mean?

One interpretation was that, at the Reformation, there was no desire to sever the Church of England from her Catholic roots but only to reform and to return to the faith as revealed in Scripture and in the received traditions of the early, undivided Church. Another interpretation, much favoured by proponents, was one promoted by certain seventeenth and eighteenth century historians. Unlike Bishop Jewel and Archbishop Laud, they claimed that the Church of England was an innovation with unrestricted authority to determine her own faith and order. Unable to evaluate the historical merits of these interpretations, many of our congregations, who have inherited the Englishman's deep seated mistrust of Rome, favoured the latter. This, together with Rome's failure to recognize the validity of Anglican Orders, meant that the 'Catholic' claims of Archbishop Fisher, that "We have no doctrine of our own; we only possess the Catholic doctrine enshrined in the Catholic creeds and those creeds we hold with no addition or diminution. On this rock we stand,"[8] went unheard; the comment attributed to Bishop Hensley Henson that, "the only doctrine peculiar to the Church of England is that there is no doctrine peculiar to the Church of England," also failed to carry weight. Many did not perceive that, forgetful of the rock from which she was hewn, the Church of England was in grave danger of becoming a Church uncertain of her authority, unclear about her doctrine and unsure about her claim to possess the historic ministry.

The very comprehensiveness of the Church of England was in itself another difficulty. It seemed feasible to assume that, as she permitted such varieties of practice and degrees of belief and churchmanship, the inclusion of women priests would extend her boundaries even further. That some would deny the validity of the orders of women priests did not seem to be a problem when the legislation included conscience clauses. What was ignored was that the Church of England was held together by her commonly accepted ministry. Any violation of this causes disruption, as John Wesley's action in ordaining ministers demonstrated. The sacramental risk this created has proved impossible to heal, even to the present day. Only when the legislation was passed by the General Synod did many of our congregations wake up to the implications of belonging to a Church in which the orders of some of its priests,and the validity of the Eucharists they would celebrate,would not be recognized by some of its members.

The Church of England's comprehensiveness also meant that there was no common understanding of the priesthood. This led to even more perplexity on the part of people in the pew. Many did not even really come to terms with the fact that to reject women priests was not to vote against the ministry of women. Furthermore, Evangelicals who would not under any circumstances have referred to their own incumbents as 'priests' or recognized them as such, voted "to make provision for the ordination of women as priests." Their concept of priesthood was totally different from that of the Anglo-Catholics in the neighbouring parish. Yet, as long as there was a commonly accepted ministry, these two extreme views could be contained and the Church held together.

Was this issue merely a matter of 'order' or a matter of 'doctrine'? Did 'order' reflect doctrine? Often, laypeople were left to think this through for themselves. Any doubt expressed about the authority of the Church of England to make the change, if it were a matter of doctrine, was often dismissed with the claim that the ordination of women was an example of "doctrinal development". This was a term used lightly and unadvisedly by speakers at all levels of the debate, but few, if asked, could have accurately defined it.

A deep and genuine desire for the unity of the Church permeated the debate at every stage but, deciding how this could best be promoted, presented the people in the pew with yet another dilemma. To vote for the legislation would facilitate a closer union with the Churches of the Anglican Communion who had in recent years decided to ordain women but would jeopardise the longstanding and developing relationships and convergence with the Roman and the Orthodox Churches. Despite the modern tendency to look towards Europe, many English people still have family ties and feel a close affinity with those who live in the former colonies, so the Anglican Communion is important. Yet the Church of England is also part of the One, Holy Catholic Church and 75% of the world's Christians are either Orthodox or Roman Catholic. Awareness of this fact seemed less acute in the English Church in the Twentieth Century than it was in Anglo Saxon times. In 664, the Church in this country faced a problem about the dating of Easter, no less divisive an issue for those Christians than the one which faces the Church at present. The Venerable Bede records that the situation was remedied by a Synod at Whitby, at which Bishop Wilfrid, who opposed the tendency of the English Church to go its own way, said, "We have seen the same customs generally observed through Italy and Gaul and in many different countries throughout the world, wherever the Church of God has spread. The only people stupid enough to disagree with the whole world are these Scots and their obstinate supporters, the Britons, who inhabit two islands in the remote ocean. Do you imagine," asked Wilfrid, "that the customs observed in a remote island are to be preferred before the customs of the Church of Christ throughout the world?"[9] At that Synod, "all present upheld the teaching of the decrees of the universal Church," and, continued Bede, "All present, both high and low, signified their agreement, and so the universal nature of the English Church was preserved." In 1984, Archbishop Runcie, with an understanding of the Church similar to that of Bishop Wilfrid, affirmed, "I was ordained a priest of the Church of God, not the 'Church of England', and our holy orders are that which we share with the whole Church. Therefore we need to look at the whole Church when we are considering this."[10]

These two quotations illustrate yet another aspect of the debate which puzzled some laypeople. When Catholic–minded opponents of the legislation were challenged with the question, "If the Roman Church were to ordain women priests, would you accept them?", the answer was usually "Yes" on the grounds that there would then be a wider consensus. Others, however, both Catholic and Evangelical, who opposed women priests, were "impossibilists", some "inopportunists", some questioned the legislation itself and others felt that the time was not ripe. The variety of reasons and motives expressed by the opponents was a cause for concern amongst some people in the pew. The proponents were unanimous and positive in their support of the legislation. There were no 'ifs' and 'buts' in their arguments. However, on a matter which is still a disputed question in the Church at large and which, even in the Church of England, is still deemed to be a subject on which different views may be held with integrity, uncertainty was to be expected. It could also be an asset if the issues highlighted by the legislation are to be properly understood.

The weakness of the Synodical system at Deanery level caused further difficulties for the laity. The parish and not the Deanery is the natural unit of English Church life and persuading people to represent their P.C.C.'s on the local Synod, especially in country areas, is hard work. Those who do are either the "activists" or public–spirited men and women who offer to "fill the gap" but have little real interest in Church politics beyond the parochial boundary.

Faced with what seemed an impossible choice, swayed first by one speaker, then by another, many of the laity were strongly influenced by their Diocesan Bishops or local clergy, a large number of whom were known to be "in favour" of the legislation.

Furthermore, the debates at Deanery level were often subjective with a woman deacon proposing the motion. The letters received by members of Diocesan and General Synod reflected that people's opinions had been formed by their experiences of the commitment and effectiveness of the work of women deacons. There was no doubt that the gifts of these women had to be used in the service of the Church. A way of achieving this had to be found but so many laypeople were unaware of the principles of Anglicanism which were undermined by this particular legislation and were unprepared for the shattering effect it is having upon the Church of England.

In Westminster Abbey, on the tombstone of the late Dr Eric Abbott, a former Dean, the simple inscription reads:

"He loved the Church of England".

Those who share that deeply rooted affection inevitably feel a terrible sense of loss as they stand by and watch what they perceive to be the very essence of that Church in danger of destruction. Bishop Gore once commented that, "The Church of England is an ingeniously devised organisation for defeating the objects it is supposed to promote." The leglislation for the ordination of women now before Parliament has the propensity to defeat a number of those objects. Members of the Church of

England must therefore be prepared to face up to the anomalies of the present and the ambiguities of the future. They must acclimatise themselves to the prospect of living within a disunited Church but with a clear and sympathetic understanding of the issues which divide them.

**Notes**

1. In Stubbs' letter to J R Green 1871: Letters of Stubbs (1904).
2. Mr Michael Hughes representing the Diocese of Salisbury, General Synod 11 November 1992.
3. Statement by the House of Bishops following the meeting in Manchester, January 1993.
4. John 16:13.
5. John 14:26.
6. Acts of the Apostles 15:15-18.
7. *'God Alive'* Darton, Longman and Todd.
8. Speech in Central Hall, Westminster 1951, quoted by Dom Anselm Hughes in *'Rivers of the Flood'*.
9. *Bede's History of the English Church and People*, Penguin Classics.
10. In a speech in the General Synod 1984.

# II

# From Reform to Retreat: Declining Authority in the Church of England

## Peter Newman Brooks

Those who write diaries will already have recorded 17 February, 1993, as a key date in the contemporary history of the Church of England. For on that fateful Wednesday, in the wake of last November's controversial vote to admit women as 'priests', almost a hundred dissident Members left a session of their Synod to meet in Westminster's Central Hall. If the media naturally made such an event something of a cabaret item on the One O'Clock News, it was cold comfort for Church historians who clearly recognized a prelude to schism. For while Church House debated liturgy, the business before the anti-Synod gathering was the nature of decision-making itself as traditionalist clergy of conviction and courage agonized over the majority vote they are clear must reduce a catholic communion of faithful people to mere sectarian status in mainstream Christendom. Such isolation their leaders still seek to prevent, and with the historic stance of the Church of England in mind, an appeal has been made to Her Majesty in the forlorn hope that, as 'Supreme Governor', Elizabeth II will intervene before it is too late. The Queen has long supported the work of the Additional Curates' Society whose Secretary, a certain Canon

Prescott, when reminding his royal Patron of the Church's lawful foundation in:

> the authority of Scripture, the XXXIX Articles, the *Book of Common Prayer* and the Ordinal

saw fit to inform Her Majesty that many felt 'perplexed and betrayed' by a Church that 'has seen fit to abandon ... historic foundations in favour of passing secular fashion'. By any standards, this is a grave charge and such an appeal unquestionably demands the most careful consideration from all lawful authority.

\* \* \* \* \*

The English Reformation of the sixteenth century secured the repudiation of papal authority over two provinces of the Western Church. At first, this meant not so much the rejection of traditional beliefs, but rather a determined bid to embrace the apostolic faith of primitive Christendom. It was an idealist attempt to recapture the remote past, all the enthusiasms of a new literacy motivating the faithful to search the scriptures, gloss patristic texts and find evidence of consensus on many controverted issues raised in early Church Councils. In such a looking-glass reformers beheld a Christian community they felt they could admire for its pristine purity. And, as many chose to stress, what they saw was a household of faith that bore little or no resemblance to the papal church of their own day. Yet in an age of authority, no such vision glorious could be realized without fundamental reform, a shaking of the foundations most felt to be attainable only if a national Prince replaced the universal Pontiff. Accordingly, and not for the first time in the intellectual history of Europe, scholars searched scriptures and the early Fathers for texts that, by enhancing the role of the 'godly prince', diminished the papal office to make its lordly incumbent merely 'bishop of Rome'. Despite the panoply of universalist power assembled at the Imperial Diet of Worms, it was Martin Luther's Elector who, albeit by anonymity and stealth, saved an obdurate professor and frightened reformer from incarceration and the stake. The object lesson proved of real value to those who sought independence, for the episode encouraged many to oppose a rudimentary nationalism to the universalist pretensions of both Empire and Papacy, claims they no longer felt to be overriding.

Although among the first to write a tract against the heresies of Doctor Martinus, dynastic considerations obliged Henry VIII to secure the succession for the House of Tudor. In a carefully calculated move that owed as much to period 'think-tank' research and the administrative genius of Thomas Cromwell as it did to his own bluster, Henry achieved this in an Act of Supremacy. By such means, English statute law effectively made the king 'pope' over the provinces of Canterbury and York, and once the 'Reformation Parliament' had secured the State against the claims of Rome, the royal conscience goaded Henry the 'godly prince' and lay theologian to pay due heed to the spiritual condition of an English Church now peculiarly subject to his oversight. In the form of Articles, *Bishops'* and *The King's Book*, Henry imposed various formularies on his subjects to indicate the orthodoxy of an independent catholicism which nonetheless continued to cherish historic creeds and prayers, commandments and sacraments, as fundamental to Christian faith. The careful phrasing and rewording of successive Henrician formularies make such public documents as fascinating as the many private catechisms and primers in circulation. Both provide abundant evidence of doctrinal division in a period when leading churchmen of traditionalist and 'protestant' persuasion joined in battle to validate conflicting orthodoxies. For the relentless process of ongoing debate and dreary polemic was no mere scholarly rivalry but a principled fight to the death with leadership of the English Church as the prize. The fabric of Tudor religion comprised a close weave and marked colour contrast, and despite the sound texture of the cloth, a confused criss-cross of conservative and radical threads obscured the overall pattern.

Henry VIII's 'catholicism without the pope' certainly delayed

Archbishop Cranmer's reforms by a decade. Nevertheless, under Edward VI, many of the Tudor Primate's pastoral priorities succeeded, and the *Book of Common Prayer* transformed the priests' Latin Mass into a Communion all the people could understand in their own tongue. Like the Act of Supremacy before it, the new liturgy was enforced at law, but the untimely demise of her half-brother enabled the new Queen to repeal the Act of Uniformity and restore the Mass. The move was itself short-lived for in her turn 'Mary the Catholic' had a limited reign, and in 1558/9 Elizabeth I brought back at law a Church both catholic and reformed. Through long years of tumult, leading lay and spiritual members of the Council had deferred to the Tudor idea of the 'godly prince'–a doctrine carefully set in place as the very foundation stone of the State Church. Although many revisionist scholars are currently at work over-painting the canvas, the landscape itself rarely changes and whether achieved in the first, or by the third, decade of her reign, Elizabeth secured an establishment united against heresy and defiant of Roman sleights of schism. Its theory proved compelling, and the *Apology* John Jewel published 'for the change of religion among us, and our departure from the church of Rome' justified the breach on similar grounds to those John Calvin adduced in his *Reply to Sadolet* (1539). For in that classic defence of reformed faith in the Swiss City State, the exiled Calvin repudiated the Cardinal's indictment of a Genevan Church in a state of schism. Rather, the Reformer urged with startling clarity, was sixteenth-century Rome itself in a sorry state of schism with the primitive Church of the apostles.

Nowadays matters are not so straightforward. Establishment is decidedly out of fashion, and as liberalism increasingly dilutes traditional Church of England doctrine, even committed anti-Catholics have begun to reconsider their position. But if, like Aunt Etty in Gwen Raverat's *Period Piece*, they 'could SWALLOW the Pope of Rome', this is a uniquely contemporary conclusion. In Elizabethan England by contrast neither Richard Hooker nor John Jewel had such stomach. Hooker's magisterial prose when he wrote:

> By the goodness of almighty God and his servant Elizabeth we are

is as meaningful as it is memorable. And Jewel's own gratitude for the salvation Royal Supremacy extended to the Church of England was both eulogistic and, in his recollection of Marian reaction, realistic in its opposition to the papal bull urging the deposition of Gloriana.

> The greatest blessing which God giveth to any people is a godly prince to rule over them. The greatest misery that can fall upon a people is to have a godly prince taken from them. [P[arker[ S[ociety], *Jewel III, 1153.]*

Equally influential too was the potent establishment theory of *Acts & Monuments*, a Church historian's *magnum opus* in which, aping Eusebius, John Foxe effectively canonized and set Constantine's name in lights for the protection and example the Roman Emperor had afforded the Early Church in an age of persecution.

But if Royal Supremacy safeguarded the provinces of Canterbury and York from submission to papal authority in Rome, could the English Church justify its claim to continuity and catholicity of belief? The very nature of ministry was central to such debate. Henry VIII had himself deplored Luther's idea of priesthood for all believers, and, written in defence of Rome's traditional seven sacraments, his *Assertio* (1521) had particularly scorned the Wittenberg Reformer's emphasis on assurance at all costs. For as part of his denunciation of 'reserved cases', Luther had advocated that, *in extremis*, confession might be made to a woman. Scholars may have reason enough to deny Henry authorship of the whole tract, but his input need not be questioned at the point where Luther is made to face the full force of royal ridicule from one with so wide an experience of the fair sex:

> . . . if anyone is mad enough to believe with Luther that

he ought to confess to a woman, perhaps it may not be amiss to follow Luther's other opinion when he persuades us not to be too careful in recalling our sins. For certainly it is not altogether convenient to be too anxious in examining your memory for what you are to put into such a person's ear, who has so large and passable a road from her ear to her tongue.

Unlike continental patterns, the English Reformers largely retained traditional forms of ministry. Rome's seven sorts of clerical status were admittedly reduced to three, but Cranmer's 'Ordinal' of 1550, revised and reissued in the second *Book of Common Prayer* (1552), carefully preserved the historic ministry of bishop, priest and deacon. The reformed liturgy laid down careful forms for the admission, by the laying on of hands, of suitably qualified men to these three grades. No mention was made of women, although in a tract of 1531, William Tyndale had tried the patience of Thomas More on that subject. In 1529, More published a *Dialogue* in which he defended the kind of popular piety Erasmus and Luther so readily attacked. From what might well have been his own past as a Lollard, Tyndale's *Answer* (1531) stressed that nothing must be allowed to obscure the preaching of the gospel. It followed that as 'women now christen and minister the sacrament of baptism in time of need', if a woman found herself on an island in what, since Golding, can be described as a *Lord-of-the-Flies* situation, 'why might she not, by the same reason, minister the sacrament of the body and blood of Christ, and teach them how to choose officers and ministers?' [P.S. *Tyndale* III, 18]

Despite the celebrated 'Nag's Head Fable', the authorities allowed no such speculative approach when Matthew Parker was chosen for Canterbury in 1559. In full accord with the hallowed traditions of the Western Church, three bishops duly consecrated Elizabeth's first Primate, and the greatest care was taken to secure apostolic continuity. Jewel thus made much of:

divers degrees of ministers in the church; whereof some be

deacons, some priests, some bishops; to whom is committed the office to instruct the people, and the whole charge and setting forth of religion. [P.S. *Jewel* III, 59]

At ordination, scriptural instruments replaced Rome's chalice and paten for priests, the whole commissioning authority directly relating to the preaching and teaching of the Christian gospel. Accordingly, any Levitical language was but loosely used, and even Whitgift held the word 'priest' to be ambiguously applied in the New Testament dispensation. At Oxford, Hugh Latimer had urged in disputation with Smith and Weston that:

> A minister is a more fit name for that office; for the name of a priest importeth a sacrifice. [P.S. *Latimer* II, 264]

For much the same reason too, Nicholas Ridley had stressed that the principal apostles were not priests 'of a popish order'. In the *Brief Declaration of the Lord's Supper* (1553) he wrote in prison, reference to the 'Ordinal' is certainly specific:

> as for the sacramental words of the order of priesthood ['Take thou authority to sacrifice ...'], I ween Peter and Paul (if they were both alive) were not able to prove, that ever Christ gave them such authority ... [P.S. *Ridley*, 19]

Jewel too was clear that:

> according to the judgement of the Nicene council...the bishop of Rome hath no more jurisdiction over the church of God than the rest of the patriarchs.

It followed that:

> except he do his duty as he ought to do, except he minister the sacraments...instruct the people...warn them and teach them...he ought not of right once to be called a bishop or so much as an elder. [P.S. *Jewel* III, 60]

Denied the right to defend themselves at the Council of Trent, most continental Reformers did little to repudiate the papal charge of heresy. Not so John Jewel who 'thought it good' for the Church of England 'to yelde up an accoumpte of oure faith in writing'. This he did at some length not only in the celebrated *Apology*, but also in a detailed *Defence* of that position against Thomas Harding, his former Oxford rival, the leader of the recusant cause in exile at Louvain. Determined to uphold the catholicity of a reformed English Church, Jewel made every effort to:

> shew it plain, that God's holy gospel, the ancient bishops and the primitive church do make our side, and that we have not without just cause left these men, and rather have returned to the apostles and old catholic fathers . . . [Ibid, 56].

Dense thickets of thorny argument followed, and against those who claimed the English Church to be 'but new and yesterday's work', the Bishop of Salisbury demanded to know, from those who 'brag so of the names of the ancient fathers, and of the new and old councils', by what authority the papacy made a whole range of claims? A devastating answer to the Roman charge of schism, the passage demands quotation in full not only for the intrinsic worth of a period purpose, but also because nowadays the text is hard to find. So therefore heed Jewel:

> Tell us, I pray you, good holy father, seeing you do crack so much of all antiquity, and boast yourself that all men are bound to you alone, which of all the fathers have at any time called you by the name of the highest prelate, the universal bishop, or the head of the church? Which of them ever said that both the swords were committed to you? Which of them ever said that you have authority and a right to call councils? Which of them ever said that the whole world is but your diocese? Which of them, that all bishops have received of your fulness? Which of them that

all power is given to you as well in heaven as in earth? Which of them, that neither kings, nor the whole clergy, nor yet all people together, are able to be judges over you? Which of them, that kings and emperors by Christ's commandment and will do receive authority at your hand? Which of them with so precise and mathematical limitation have surveyed and determined you to be seventy and seven times greater than the mightiest kings? Which of them, that more ample authority is given to you than the residue of the patriarchs? Which of them, that you are the Lord God? or that you are not a mere natural man, but a certain substance made and grown together of God and man? Which of them, that you are the only head- spring of all law? Which of them, that you have power over purgatories? Which of them, that you are able to command the angels of God as you list yourself? Which of them that ever said, that you are Lord of lords and the King of kings? We can also go further with you in like sort. What one amongst the whole number of the old bishops and fathers ever taught you, either to say private mass whiles the people stared on, or to lift up the sacrament over your head (in which point now consisteth all your religion); or else to mangle Christ's sacraments, and to bereave the people of the one part, contrary to Christ's institution and plain expressed words? But, that we may once come to an end, what one is there of all the fathers which hath taught you to distribute Christ's blood and the holy martyrs' merits, and to sell openly as merchandises your pardons and all the rooms and lodgings of purgatory? [P.S. *Jewel* III, 88]

Such merit in 'the good old cause' now has a hollow ring, and strikes few chords in the ears of members of the Church of England. Yet in half a century when Rome itself has undergone significant reform, instead of trying to heal the sadness of past schism, English Synods–all too often dominated by new-style ecclesiastical fashions–seem instead to seek its aggravation.

The gravitational shift that once resulted in reform of an overly Roman religion has now been reversed. Liberal interpretations of scripture, calculated ridicule of creeds, and lamentable liturgical change have successively compromised and weakened the doctrinal position of an historic part of the Church of Christ. Further synodical absurdity will certainly bring tragic schism and disastrous retreat into sectarianism. It is a daunting prospect, and a great pity contemporary churchmen and women cannot content themselves by building on past strengths. A sense of history would certainly help all to realize, if further apology is needed, the relevance of some last words from John Jewel:

> Now-a-days the holy scripture is abroad, the writings of the apostles and prophets are in print, whereby all truth and catholic doctrines may be proved, and all heresy disproved and confounded. [Ibid, III, 57]

# III

# A Vote for Variance: Continuity, Change and the Catholicity of Anglicanism

## Geoffrey Rowell

'Ye shall pray for Christ's Holy Catholic Church, that is for the whole congregation of Christian people dispersed throughout the whole world....' So run the words of the bidding prayer used before University Sermons in Oxford, following the form set out in Canon 55 of the Canons of 1604. In the Second Book of Homilies (1571) the 'true Church of Christ' is contrasted with the contemporary Church of Rome.

'The true Church is a universal congregation or fellowship of God's faithful and elect people, *built upon the foundation of the Apostles and Prophets, Jesus Christ himself being the head corner stone.* And it hath always three notes or marks, whereby it is known; pure and sound doctrine, the Sacraments ministered according to Christ's holy institution, and the right use of ecclesiastical discipline. This description of the Church is agreeable both to the Scriptures of God and also to the doctrine of the ancient fathers, so that none may justly find fault therewith.'[1] The Church of Rome, which was faithful to Christ at the beginning, is now held to have erred by ordering the Sacraments and discipline of the Church, not 'in such sort' as Christ 'did first institute and ordain them,' but by an intermingling of 'their own traditions and inventions, by chopping and changing, by adding and plucking away, that now they may seem to have been converted into a new guise.'[2]

It was the intention of the Anglican reformers to order the Church of England so that it conformed more closely in its polity and worship to the Church established by Christ, grounded in Scripture, and obedient to the faith and order of the Church of the early centuries. The Nicene and Apostles' Creeds, together with the *Quincunque vult* (the so-called 'Athanasian Creed'), were given a prominent place in Anglican worship. The three-fold ministry of bishops, priests and deacons was maintained in direct historic continuity with the ministry Christ gave to his apostles. There was no intention of changing or repudiating that ministry and its apostolic succession, whatever polemic there may have been against contemporary understandings of priesthood in popular Catholicism. Richard Hooker, perhaps the greatest of all Anglican divines, argued cogently against contemporary Puritans for the place of bishops in the Church. Hooker recognised the need of the Church to adapt to changing circumstances, and believed that the Church had power to make provision for new forms of worship.

'All things cannot be of ancient continuance, which are expedient and needful for the ordering of spiritual affairs: but the Church being a body which dieth not hath always power, as occasion requireth no less to ordain that which never was, than to ratify that which was before.' 'Laws touching matter of order,' writes Hooker, 'are changeable, by the power of the Church; articles concerning doctrine not so.'[3] Despite the use of the word 'order', what Hooker has in mind is liturgy and orders of service not the order of ministry, and even regarding the former the controlling principle must be that which points the worshipper to heaven, and which embodies respect for what has been handed down from the formative centuries of the Christian Church.[4] Hooker after all devotes much space to an exposition of the apostolic basis of episcopacy against Puritan detractors. Although, as Article XXXIV states 'every particular or national Church hath authority to ordain, change and abolish, ceremonies or rites of the Church ordained only by man's authority,' such authority is carefully limited by warnings against not offending against the common order of the Church, hurting the consciences of the weak brethren, doing all for the edifying (building up) of the Church, and doing nothing as of enforced requirement that has not the warranty of Scripture.

Article XX, which was cited by the Archbishop of Canterbury in his speech in the November 11th debate, states that 'the Church hath power to decree Rites and Ceremonies, and authority in Controversies of Faith.' Yet the preceding article warns that the churches of Jerusalem, Alexandria, Antioch and Rome have erred 'not only in their living and manner of Ceremonies, but also in matters of faith.' And the following article stresses that General Councils 'may err and sometimes have erred, even in things pertaining unto God.' For that reason, Article XXI continues, 'things ordained by them as necessary to salvation have neither strength nor authority, unless it may be declared that they be taken out of holy Scripture.' Article XIX, after defining the Church of Christ as 'a congregation of faithful men, in which the pure Word of God is preached, and the Sacraments...duly ministered', defines the mode of that ministration as 'according to Christ's ordinance in all those things that of necessity are requisite to the same.' The Church is bound to Scripture and to apostolic faith, ministry and sacramental practice. The Worship and Doctrine Measure, which gave the General Synod authority to decide matters 'touching' doctrine, was careful to cite the canon defining the doctrine of the Church of England as grounded in Holy Scripture, the ancient Fathers and Councils agreeable to Scripture, and the historic formularies of the Book of Common Prayer and the ordering of Bishops, Priests and Deacons. The declaration of assent made at ordinations and institutions begins with the affirmation that the Church of

England is part of the 'One, Holy, Catholic and Apostolic Church'.... 'professing the faith uniquely revealed in the Holy Scriptures, and set forth in the catholic creeds, and to which the historic formularies of the Church of England bear witness.' Anglican faith and order are clearly bound first to the test of Scripture, then to the early Fathers and Councils, and finally to the Prayer Book and the Ordinal. This was (and is) intended as a safeguard of the apostolic faith and order and the catholic continuity of Anglicanism. The Reformation was never intended to be innovation, but, to use a phrase that has been used of the Oxford Movement, to be a 'revolution by tradition.' The disputes about ministry and sacraments among the Reformation churches were about the scriptural evidence and grounding for particular practices. Amongst those Reformation churches the Church of England (along with many Lutheran churches) was conservative of its catholic continuity and identity, while protesting against Roman innovations. Since that time Rome has undergone two significant reformations of its own–the 'counter-Reformation' of the sixteenth century and the *aggiornamento* of the Second Vatican Council. The latter, as we know, has made possible the considerable degree of theological convergence represented by the ARCIC documents.

It is not denied by those who argued for the ordination of women to the priesthood, whether in the Synod debate or before, that it is an innovation. The Archbishop of Canterbury said it was 'a development in the Church's tradition.'[5] The Bishop of Guildford, more curiously, claimed that tradition required it–a point rebutted by the Bishop of Newcastle. 'Surely it is quite misleading to enlist tradition without qualification in favour of this legislation, for it is at this very point that the arguments in favour of the legislation are at their weakest.' At the most tradition through its silence in word (though not in practice) can only lead to a '"not proven" or a straight "no".'[6]

The Church of England and the Anglican Communion have undertaken major ecumenical dialogues with the two great communions of East and West which make up by far the larger part of Christendom. Although there are pressures within the

Roman Catholic Church for the ordination of women, the clear and continuing response at the level of the official dialogue, and from the magisterium of the Papacy, is that this constitutes 'a new, grave and serious obstacle,' and is a development that is not consonant with scripture and tradition. The Roman Catholic position is summed up in the 1980 Lutheran-Roman Catholic statement, *All One in Christ*, that 'the Catholic church according to its practice and doctrine does not see itself in a position to admit women to ordination.'[7] The new *Catechism of the Catholic Church* puts it tersely:

> Only a baptised man can validly receive sacred ordination. The Lord Jesus chose men to form the college of the twelve apostles, and the apostles did the same when they chose those co-workers to succeed them in their task. The college of bishops, with whom the presbyters are united in the priesthood, makes the college of the twelve an ever-present reality until Christ's return. The Church considers herself bound by this choice of the Lord. For this reason the ordination of women is not possible.[8]

The Athens Statement of the Anglican/Orthodox Joint Doctrinal Commission of 1978 was a direct endeavour to meet the ecumenical difficulties caused by the ordination of women in the Anglican Communion. The Orthodox stated (1) that men and women, made in the image of God, have a diversity of functions and gifts, which are complementary, but not all interchangeable; (2) the ordination of women to the priesthood is an innovation, lacking any basis whatever in Holy Tradition; (3) that Tradition is living and creative, but this innovation is not part of that creative continuity but a breach of apostolic faith and order; (4) those Orthodox churches which have 'partially or provisionally recognised Anglican Orders' did so on the grounds that Anglicans had preserved the apostolic succession in ministry, faith and spiritual life–the ordination of women by varying this calls the apostolic identity of Anglicanism into question. The Anglican statement recognised a diversity of views and asked a series of questions:

> How far in such questions should consensus precede ac-
> tion; how far may the experience of such actions itself lead
> to a new consensus? What methods of decision and debate
> are appropriate in such matters? Should the Synods of
> particular Church provinces have the freedom to make
> decisions in matters which affect not only the whole
> Anglican Communion, but also our relations with all other
> Churches? Is the traditional Anglican claim to have no
> specifically Anglican Scriptures, Creeds, Sacraments and
> Ministry but only those of the universal Church put in
> jeopardy by actions of this kind? What is the ecclesiologi-
> cal significance of the fact that we now have a ministry
> not universally recognised within our own Communion?
> Where does our authority in such matters lie?[9]

Catholic Anglicans have always emphasised the continuity and
identity of the Anglican ministry with the historic ministry of the
Church. Anglicans are ordained as bishops, priests, and deacons
'in the Church of God'–not of the Church of England, or any
other local Church of the Anglican Communion. They have
welcomed the moves towards recognition of Anglican Orders by
the Orthodox churches between the two World Wars. They
stood firmly behind the response of the Archbishops of Canterbury and York to the Papal condemnation of Anglican orders in
the Bull, *Apostolicae Curae* in 1896, and saw in the agreement
on Ministry in the ARCIC I conversations a major rappproche-
ment between Roman Catholics and Anglicans which pointed
the way to a reconsideration of the verdict of 1896. Archbishop
Whitgift's contention in his response to the Puritan Thomas
Cartwright that the Church had been reformed according to
Scripture and the ancient traditions and not transformed into
something new,[10] and Archbishop Bramhall's contention a century later that the tradition received by the Church of England
consisted partly in *credenda*, articles of belief, and partly of
*agenda*, things done, are early Anglican witnesses to a long-

standing affirmation of Anglican identity with the church of the Fathers, an identity symbolised by the careful preservation of the historic threefold ministry.

The questions posed by the Anglican delegates in Athens in 1978 have remained pertinent but have scarcely been seriously addressed. The Synod vote of November 11th now brings home to the Church of England the question posed more generally about the Anglican Communion—'What is the ecclesiological significance of the fact that we now have a ministry not universally recognised within our Communion?' For the nub of the question is that dubious orders have been created by a unilateral action. For such orders to be assured (and therefore to be fully received within the Church) Catholic consent and consensus is needed. It is manifestly clear that this simply does not exist, whether you turn to our Orthodox and Roman Catholic brothers and sisters, or whether you look at the Church of England alone. The January meeting of the House of Bishops this year (1993), endeavoured to respond to the division created by the Synod vote. They have promised that those who do not believe the Synod had authority to act contrary to Catholic order, practice and consensus, will have a permanent and protected place within the Church of England, and that there will be a sufficiency of bishops (regional and provincial) to minister to them. The attempt to comprehend within the ministry of the Church of England women priests whose orders will not be recognised by a percentage of their fellow priests and a considerable number of the laity may be viewed as either a praiseworthy endeavour to live with a disputed issue, or the inauguration of something doomed to failure. Church history does not give us any encouragement to think that a church can live with such a divided ministry and impaired communion. The practicalities of deaneries, cathedrals and dioceses—of every context in which clergy must needs meet together—demonstrate how fraught and difficult such situations may be. Bishops who are opposed, because they hold a theology and an ecclesiology which means that the ordination of women to the priesthood is a disputed question in the light of scripture and tradition, cannot in integrity either ordain or licence women priests. Their guardianship of the faith and order of the church means that, however charitable they may wish to be towards the women whom the Church of England has decided to ordain to the priesthood, they cannot share with them and delegate to them a cure of souls, where by so doing they would be introducing into that parish in their diocese those whose orders they believe to be dubious, and who therefore introduce into the heart of the church's eucharistic life doubt at the very point at which assurance is vital and necessary. The Archdeacon of Leicester made this point strongly in the Synod debate when he asked the pertinent question, 'can there be anything provisional about a ministry on which depend the sacraments of the Church?'[11]

Among the opponents of the ordination of women are those who believe that the unvarying tradition of the Church, and the lack of clear Scripture support for women's ordination, means that this is never an option for the Church. Others, while recognising that clear historical givenness, may acknowledge that there are important questions to be addressed by all the churches relating to the place of women in the church, the mystery of masculinity and femininity, and the relation of that mystery to the mystery of priesthood. (The discussion group of Anglican, Orthodox and Roman Catholic men and women in which I took part, and whose report *A Fearful Symmetry* (SPCK) was published some weeks before the Synod vote, indicates how subtle and complex the issues are). For Catholics in this position the question is not an open and closed one, but they are still caught in the dilemma that to enact what is dubious because of lack of catholic consensus is to introduce doubt at the heart of the sacramental life of the church. They have a greater reverence for the unbroken tradition of the church, than for arguments deployed over little more than two decades. 'Proceed with caution' may not be cowardly but pastorally and theologically responsible. And it scarcely need be said that if a vote to ordain women to the priesthood has caused such deep division within the church, then a subsequent vote to enable women to be bishops would be fatally so. Yet that is, of course, the situation in two provinces of the Anglican Communion.

In summary Catholic Anglicans following the vote are faced with a church which has:

(1) called into question its claim to have no distinctive doctrines, and has acted unilaterally to alter the universal historic ministry of the church;

(2) willed to bring into being orders which, because of lack of catholic consent, and firm grounding in scripture and tradition, are dubious, and which therefore import doubt into the heart of the sacramental life of the church;

(3) moved away from its own foundation formularies by opting to enact a new development of doctrine, despite its own division on the matter, and ecumenical warnings;

(4) thereby impaired its own life and communion, as well as erecting a new ecumenical barrier;

(5) by doing this raised questions about its own understanding of Christianity as a revealed religion, handed on from generation to generation  by bonds of common faith and order.

**Notes**

1. (J.Griffiths (ed.)), *The Two Books of Homilies appointed to be read in Churches*, Oxford, 1859, p.462, Homily for Whitsunday.
2. Ibid.
3. Richard Hooker, *The Laws of Ecclesiastical Polity*, V. viii. 2.
4. Ibid., V.vi.2; V.vii.1.
5. *The Ordination of Women to the Priesthood: The Synod Debate, 11 November 1992, The Verbatim Record*, 1993, p.23.
6. Ibid., pp.10, 41.
7. H. Meyer and L. Vischer (ed.), *Growth in Agreement: Reports and Agreed Statements of Ecumenical Conversations on a World Level*, 1984, p.256.
8. *Catechism of the Catholic Church*, 1993 s. 1577.
9. Meyer and Vischer, op.cit., pp.51-53.
10. J.Whitgift, *The Defence of the Answer to the Admonition against the Reply of Thomas Cartwright, Works*, II, (Parker Society, 1852), p.439; J.Bramhall, *Schism Guarded, and beaten back upon the right owners, shewing that our great controversy about Papal power is not a question of faith but of interest and profit; not with the Church of Rome but with the court of Rome; wherein the true controversy doth consist; who were the first innovators; when and where these Papal innovations first began in England; with the opposition that was made against them, Works*, II, (Library of Anglo-Catholic Theology, 1852), pp. 470-1.
11. *The Ordination of Women to the Priesthood: Synod Debate*, pp. 12-13.

# IV

# The Issue of Authority

## G. R. Evans

The vote in favour of legislation permitting the ordination of women, taken by the General Synod of the Church of England on November 11th, 1992, has raised new issues about authority. Some of these have the potential to be ecclesiologically stimulating. That is to say, they may be valuable in clearing minds on some knotty problems which have been getting in the way ecumenically, as well as within the Church of England itself. It is accepted very widely now that we can still speak of communion even where it is impaired, and that the way forward ecumenically is to try to build on the profound reality of what we have.[1] But it is equally plain that the principal stumbling-block to the implementation of unity schemes is almost always a problem about the mutual recognition and acceptance of one another's ministerial order. We now have such a difficulty internally within the Anglican Communion, and are about to experience it at first hand within the Church of England.

Three things are brought together when a person is ordained to the ministry. There is the gift of the Holy Spirit; an act of 'order' which sets the candidate in a new relationship to the community; and the entrusting to the newly ordained minister of the duties of a particular 'office' in the community. When the General Synod voted in favour of the ordination of women to the priesthood in the Church of England, it was not clear to all those present that the Holy Spirit could be so given; it was known that women could not be set in the same relationship to the whole community as male candidates, because not all members of the community would be able to accept them; and it was clear that some local communities at parish level would certainly not accept women as their pastors so the offices open to them would be limited. But if we believe, as Anglicans do, that ordination cannot be provisional, and is for life, a body of persons ordained with the intention of making them priests on that understanding, thus comes into existence. These are people, not opinions. They are 'shared' by the community in a way particular beliefs need not be, and to differ as to whether they are priests or not is to be divided. The question is whether that division must necessarily be Church-dividing. The development of Christian ministry arose at a number of points in response to pastoral and practical need and the theological legitimacy was established only afterwards.[2] The authoritativeness of what had been done thus became retrospective.

Legislation can be changed. Among the responses there have already been calls for a resolve to fight for the reversal of what the General Synods in both countries (England and Australia) have done.[3] But that reversal is only a possibility in the interim period before the new law is acted on and ordinations take place. The crux of the matter is that a decision which cannot be reversed in any simple way[4] once the first women are ordained, has had to be taken in circumstances where it is impossible to be sure[5] on a number of points.

It is this combination of uncertainty and irreversibility which presents us with our present challenges. At the deepest level these are in keeping with the experience of the Church through the ages, which has always had to risk what has been precious to it in order to be truly at the disposal of the Holy Spirit.[6] 'The Church cannot be regarded as a kind of universal Garrick Club which exists mainly for the purpose of making its members feel content and secure in the solidity of its traditions. Rather it is a body whose founder called for the transformation of each individual's relationship to God and with the human beings through whom God is manifest to us."[7]

In what follows I have tried to distinguish two sorts of authority-problem: authority to make the decision; authority to implement it and maintain ecclesial integrity where not everyone can accept what has been decided and some want to leave the Church. This cannot be more than an interim account.[8] But it is very important for the ecclesiological consequences to be clear now as we go along.

## Authority to make the decision

The decision to approve legislation which will make it possible for women to be ordained to the priesthood has been made by the General Synod of the twin provinces of England, Canterbury and York. The Synod is, therefore, in effect, a provincial synod, and it is doing what other provincial synods in the Anglican Communion have already done. The precedent in tradition is strong. From the early Church[9] groups of diocesan bishops have met with their patriarch or primate or metropolitan to make laws for their region. The only significant modern difference is that the dioceses are now also represented in the synod by clergy and laity who have a vote alongside the bishops. These are there as elected representatives, while the bishops represent their people by virtue of the special relationship in which they are placed to the community by their ordination and pastoral office. So two kinds of 'representation' are involved.[10] This makes of the modern synod something essentially different in its authoritativeness from the older models, because it is no longer a meeting of local (diocesan) churches in their leaders, but also of individuals who may feel themselves to 'represent' interest groups cutting across ecclesial and pastoral units, as well as their local churches. The Synod's decision was also the bishops' decision. But whereas in the early Church the Synod was the bishops, it is now in the Church of England the case that the Synod could collectively take a view opposed to that of the majority of the Bishops where voting is not by Houses.

The present Archbishop of York has argued that it would have been desirable for the decision to be taken in the first instance by the House of Bishops, in its leadership and representative role, and for the other two Houses then to express the *consensus fidelium*.[11] That would certainly have been ecclesiologically tidier in its implications for the authority of the decision at a level deeper than the legislative. The process thus conducted would have made plain something which is easily lost sight of in the present synodical structure–the existence of the House of Bishops as a decision-making body in its own right, with special responsibility for leadership and guardianship of faith and order.

There has never been any question about a provincial synod's right to legislate for its own affairs.[12] The practical common sense of this is underlined by the fact that provinces are natural working units, often coinciding geographically with the secular legislatures with which they stand in relationship.[13] The ordination of women to the priesthood in other provinces of the Anglican Communion did not cause real difficulties for the Church of England. Their ordination within the Church of England will. But ancient tradition also stressed the importance of seeking to legislate unanimously within the province or metropolitan area, and of doing nothing which would break or damage communion with other Churches. When what is decided is a point touching common ministerial order we cannot just agree to differ because we cannot confine the difference to individual conscience. It affects the whole life of the Church. A decision which is not unanimous and which cannot be accepted by all, but which unavoidably affects all, does not fit tidily within the ancient boundaries limiting what provincial or metropolitan groups of dioceses might decide.

The first line of the legislation on which the November vote was taken says that women may become priests 'in the Church of England'. The Anglican principle, like that of the Roman Catholic and Orthodox Churches, has always been that ordination makes priests 'in the Church of God'. The legislation also speaks of office rather than of order. Both these points are important in relation to the question of the limits of synodical authority. Law does not ordain. It merely gives or withholds permission for certain persons to be ordained in certain circumstances and to hold pastoral charge. It therefore confines itself in this case to permitting the women that bishops ordain to be deemed priests within the Church of England and to hold office there. It thus does not claim more than has been claimed before for legislation's powers. But it does not, because it cannot, directly address the sacramental issues relating to the bestowing of priestly orders on women.[14] It must, in effect, beg the question of authority to ordain women to the priesthood, deem that to exist, and enact laws allowing it to be done in the Church of England. In other words, the proposed legislation has not made the decision that women may be priests. It takes it to have been made.

Similarly, the role of Parliament in giving legislative force to the decision from the secular side does not go beyond precedent. The Legislative Committee of the General Synod has to make a report to the Ecclesiastical Committee of Parliament, which is made up of 15 peers and 15 MPs. This Ecclesiastical Committee then decides whether the measure is 'expedient'. If it says that it is, the Priests (Ordination of Women) Measure will be debated in the Houses of Commons and Lords. If it is passed in both Houses, it goes for Royal Assent. A petition for promulgating the canons can then be made. The General Synod then has to promulgate the canons, and it is at that stage that it becomes possible for a bishop actually to ordain a woman priest.[15]

There seems no real likelihood of Parliament's blocking the decision at this stage.[16] But there are two grounds on which the authoritativeness of the Synod's decision might be challenged. There is a question about the workability of the legislation, which touches the heart of the notion of authoritativeness, if it is to be argued that right authority in the Church is essentially 'orderly'. One commentator speaks of 'the...worry that the legislation passed in its present form is unworkable and may be (in parliamentary terms) "inexpedient". That would bring its authoritativeness into question, by showing that what is proposed cannot be done."[17]

It could also be argued that legislation can be proved not to be authoritative if it is *de facto* not accepted. 'I do not think that I am the only person to have hoped that after last Wednesday, it would be accepted that the decision had been made in accordance with the structure of Synod, and that the many arguments relating to the priesting of women would end. Sadly, this does not seem to be so . . . In the name of the Lord we all attempt to serve, may I ask for acceptance of the decision, before the Church is finally torn apart,'[18] cries one Anglican. 'It now seems that the Synod cannot carry the Church with it,'[19] notes another. This is another kind of challenge to the authoritativeness of what has been done by way of decision-making, but not yet irrevocably done by way of enactment.

## Authority to implement the decision and to maintain ecclesial integrity

The results of challenge to the authority of the Synod to make the decision it has made by saying that it will not work, or simply not accepting it are likely to be manifold. Several possibilities are already suggesting themselves. It has been agreed that as far as possible the Church should be held together. The Church of England's official wish, expressed by the Archbishop of Canterbury in the debate, and by the other Bishops in their statement of 14th January, 1993, is to prevent schism. The Bishop of London, David Hope, on BBC Radio 4's World at One on 20 November said, 'We are trying to arrange for people to stay in the Church of England, not to leave it'. These claims would seem to stress the intention of the Church of England in making this decision to continue in its former catholicity.

## Negative solutions

### i. *Remaining within the Church of England but disowning episcopal oversight in certain dioceses*

Some have already said that they believe themselves already not to be under the episcopal oversight of particular bishops to whom they have hitherto owed canonical obedience. 'At a meeting convened by Canon Anthony Prescott, general secretary of the Additional Curates Society, 32 priests in the Birmingham diocese agreed that they could not continue to regard Bishop Mark Santer as their father-in-God.'[20] Others would argue the other way. 'We are not required to agree with all our bishop's opinions, or approve of all his actions, but we are bound by our ordination vows to render canonical obedience.'[21] But the fact that this disowning of bishops is under discussion by priests at all makes an ecclesiological statement. It shows that it is possible for priests holding strong views about traditional order, with its concomitant bond for a priest or deacon of obedience to his bishop, to find themselves forced in conscience to deny one area of authority in order to be faithful, as they see it, to another. Ecclesial authoritativeness is thus deemed to be composed of separable elements.

This challenge also implies the idea that bishops can become tainted and their ministry thus invalidated. That presents a challenge to authority of another sort, and one which results in a 'Donatist' type of schism. The House of Bishops insisted in its statement of January 14, 1993. 'We do not and cannot accept the theological reasoning behind the view that in some way those bishops and priests who participate in the ordination of women to the priesthood thereby invalidate their sacramental ministry'.

## ii. *Seeking guarantees*

'We want guarantees', said John Broadhurst.[22] A lack of trust of the bishops is being voiced, with calls for guarantees, enshrined in legislation not just a code of practice. This goes with an expressed fear that the long-term effect, or even plan, will be to eliminate opposition. This mistrust must be incompatible with the bond of charity which is intrinsic to right order in the Church. It is directly addressed by the House of Bishops'

statement of 14 January, 1993. 'We believe that the pastoral
arrangements which we go on to outline can help to ensure the
continued presence within posts of this nature of those with
objections to the ordination of women to the priesthood'. This
sort of thinking colours the conception of authority with which
we are dealing by seeing it as desirable that it should be rigidly
enforced rather than flexible and adaptable.

### iii. *Threatening to leave the Church of England altogether*

Some of those who throw down a more outright ecclesiological
challenge want to bring the Church of England to its senses by
threatening to leave it. This is sometimes fear expressed as
aggression. 'We must not submit to our Church being stripped
of its catholicity and take that betrayal meekly.'[23] The emphasis here may be upon 'threat', as has been apparent to
more than one commentator. Cardinal Edward Cassidy thinks
Graham Leonard's talk of going to Rome is 'appealing to
his own Church'. He 'would not read it as an appeal to
us.... I would think from his letter that he is hopeful that there
would still be movement within the Church of England'. 'There
is an illogicality about the "threats" of some Anglicans to
become Roman Catholics at some unspecified future date',
notes another commentator. 'If they are convinced that the
Roman claims... are true, then surely it is their duty to submit
today,... irrespective of what the Church of England does
about women priests or indeed anything else.... To "threaten"
or "promise" to submit in the future is neither here nor there'.[24]
Insofar as this is a matter of threat it challenges authority by
showing that that authority need not be submitted to. But it also
raises the question of the duty of charity, for threat is incompatible with brotherly love. And it throws open the question
whether those who acted upon the threat would not by doing so
constitute themselves a body united by certain demands and
capable of moving independently again.

## Positive solutions

The principle of charitable protection of the losers is like Augustine's idea that politics is necessary only because we are fallen; that is, it is necessary, because we are not unanimous, to build into the structures of the community provision to meet the needs of those who need protection. Some suggestions as to how this might be done have come from those who feel themselves to be the losers. Others are being put forward collectively by the bishops and therefore with their authority, to protect the 'losers'.

### i. *The church within a church*

Forward in Faith is a new umbrella body including Cost of Conscience, Women against the Ordination of Women, the Association for Apostolic Ministry, the Society of the Holy Cross. It has produced a statement which supports the model of a church within a church, and which doubts assurances that the position of those against the ordination of women will be fully protected. This is the implication of the call for guarantees to ensure the continuance of the Church of England within the church of England. 'There is in our view a degree of doubt sufficient to call seriously into question the orders and sacraments which would result from the promulgation of the ... canons .... in our view there will need to be an assured succession of bishops who do not ordain women to the priesthood or recognise them as priests; liberty for clergy and parishes to associate themselves for all sacramental and pastoral purposes with those bishops; and places of theological education and training for the priesthood which respect the position of those whom such bishops recommend.' 'We believe that such provision can be made within the existing structure of the Church of England.' ... 'jurisdictional problems ... will inevitably present themselves. We trust that the House of Bishops will fully recognise the impairment of communion which the promulgation of canons will entail; we hope that it will nevertheless seek to build upon the wider unity through baptism and a common spiritual heritage which will assuredly remain.'[25]

## ii. *Holding the Church of England together but altering the diocesan pattern of episcopal oversight through the provision of alternatives*

The Reformation Church Trust (about 25 members) wants to form a group to seek alternative episcopal oversight. Such alternative episcopal oversight would provide the pastoral care of a bishop for those who do not want what their diocesan offers. There could (as it looks at present) be no time-limit on this arrangement, no point at which it ceased. There is a further challenge here to the diocesan role of the bishop as understood in the Anglican, Roman Catholic and Orthodox systems. One bishop, one diocese, has always been the pattern, with suffragans, episcopal vicars, extending their diocesan's own pastoral ministry. The 'flying' bishop would have a ministry to a community of minority opinion.[26] That is without precedent.[27] But it is not intended that it should be a 'travelling' office. Such a bishop would hold an ordinary diocesan position as well, while being available to visit other dioceses. The House of Bishops stresses, however, that 'each diocesan bishop will continue to accept full responsibility for the episcopal oversight and pastoral care of all in his charge', and says 'where necessary he will extend this care in appropriate ways' (January 14, 1993).

The House of Bishops, meeting in January, 1993, has proposed a variant of this scheme in the form of three provincial episcopal visitors, whose functions would not intrude upon those of the local diocesan,[28] but who would perform for the 'traditionalists' the pastoral and sacramental functions they would not feel able to accept at the hands of their diocesan. This could be needed where there is no suffragan in the diocese to act in the ways envisaged above. This involves constructing a 'non-territorial' third province in the Church of England. There is precedent for a 'non-territorial' and figurative conception of 'locality' in the Church, notably where cultural or ethnic identity persists among immigrants or exiles,[29] but this will be envisaged in rather a different way, as an extra-ordinary provision.[30]

### iii. Remaining within the Church of England but forming a system of parishes within it which will accept the oversight of bishops of their own persuasion only.

Some suggest a solution with a geographical base but a patchwork one, 'to remain firmly within the Church of England, loyal to its timeless apostolic commission if not its transitory General Synod, and develop a federation of Catholic parishes delineated quite distinctly within the Church, served by bishops who will continue to have nothing to do with the ordination of women priests.'[31]

One problem with this, as is clear on all sides, is that there will be few if any parishes where opinion is unanimous.

It is also a major ecclesiological difficulty that the authority of the local community at parish level to be self-determining does not have the kind of precedent which can be found in the early tradition for 'provincial' autonomy. It has strong precedent in the practice of the Reformation Churches, which chose to avoid episcopacy and which continue to regard the local 'gathered' community as the sole true manifestation of the visible Church.[32] But in the episcopal tradition, the parish is a sub-unit of the diocese and its priests the bishop's vicars and assistants. The bishop delegates his pastoral ministry to the priests and the people and the parishes remain ultimately in his pastoral care.[33]

## 'Neutral' solutions

### i. Actually leaving the Church of England but retaining its rite in communion with another Church (the 'uniate' solution)

The 'uniate' solution forms an enclave which belongs to both and to neither Church. This has been put forward only tentatively. Graham Leonard has put forward a proposal to 'seek relationship with the Roman Catholic Church', 'as suppliants and without presumption, asking if a way could be found for us somehow to preserve our Anglican identity while being in communion with the See of Peter. I do not think it is for us to suggest how this might be achieved.'[34] The uniate pattern has not had an altogether happy history in Eastern Europe, [35] because it leaves an unsatisfactory sense of ecclesial belonging, and therefore of authority unresolved.

### ii. *Actually leaving the Church of England, but with its blessing, and becoming members of another Church*

The House of Bishops said in February, 1987, that 'those who could not remain in communion with the See of Canterbury would need to find other ways of continuing their existence within the universal Church and would be entitled to explore such ways'.[36] This is to give permission to go, to those who cannot in conscience stay, and to allow them to submit to ecclesial authority elsewhere within the wider Church. That is in one sense ecumenically generous. In another, it is ecumenically unhelpful partly because, like the uniate solution, it assumes a difference of catholicity between communions.

Authority to continue what has been accepted by the community over time is relatively uncontroversial; authority in a period of change is not. This is distinct from the issue of authority to make the decision which sets the train of events in motion. The legislation as it stands is designed to contain and prevent consequences of the sort just outlined. It has been criticised as setting up 'institutionalised disunity',[37] and it raises issues of its own about authority in the Church in emergency situations.

## Unauthorised gradual change

We need to underline first the fact that the present emergency situation is not seen by all those who find it so as confined to the decision to ordain women to the priesthood. A high proportion of those opposed to the decision link with it what they see as a change elsewhere in the Church of England's life. John Gummer, for example, is inclined to associate with the decision to ordain women a trend towards liberalism and abandoning the Prayer Book, and to oppose the Synod's claims to authority to the 'apostolic' authority of the episcopate. On resigning from General Synod on 1 December, 1992, he said, 'In future, "Archbishop of Canterbury" will be merely a courtesy title. Instead of being enthroned in St. Augustine's Chair as successor of the Apostles, he will sit there by courtesy of the General Synod.' ... bishops' authority will 'only derive from a two-thirds majority of what is at best a provincial synod. I cannot continue as a member of a body which pretends it has the power to make priests without authority of Scripture or tradition. The Synod has finally turned the Church of England into a sect.'[38]

It is for this double reason, that it creates an emergency situation in the Church's order and that it stirs a muddy pool of potentially negative associations for those who feel their position is not respected by current trends, that authority to preserve the Church's unity cannot operate in an altogether orderly way in the present crisis.

The inherent untidiness of the situation makes for subtle and perhaps unforeseeable change, for change which happens without its being intended. Here again we come up against echoes of the problem addressed by the call for guarantees. Women against the Ordination of Women made a statement after the November 11th vote, together with Cost of Conscience: 'We call upon our representatives in Parliament to defer the passage of any bill until effective assurances have been given that those opposed will continue to be recommended for ordination, to be eligible for posts at diocesan and national level, and to be eligible for appointment as bishops.'[39] Hugh Craig, Oxford, speaking in the November debate, was concerned at the way the legislation differentiated between present and future bishops in a way that would change the nature of bishops. If it went through, a third of the clergy would find themselves denied preferment. He thought the legislation should be less concerned with those who would want to leave the Church, and more with those who objected to women priests, but still intended to stay.[40]

The Archbishop of Canterbury made a statement that the whole House of Bishops was united in seeking to ensure that there would be no discrimination, and that the unity and integrity of the Church of England were maintained.[41] But the Bishop of London, David Hope, was not convinced by the assurances of the well-being and inclusion of those who were opposed.

We are in a position to see something of what time has been doing in other provinces of the Anglican Communion which have already been meeting the practical difficulties we now face. On the one hand reception and familiarisation can be seen to be operating to make what has been done *de facto* authoritative. This is along the lines Mark Santer has pointed to in admitting in the debate of November 11th that he used to believe that it could wait until there was greater concensus in the Church, but he now believed that to go on waiting was debilitating to the life of the Church[42]. 'In Canada, when the first women were ordained priests, there were members of the Church who disapproved. Some left, some formed a splinter group which seems to have died, and most stayed. Of those who stayed many, I would venture to say, have changed their point of view about the idea of women priests. The bishop who ordained me changed his mind completely,'[43] says a Canadian woman priest.

But at the same time there is a breakdown of common order. In the USA there are five Anglican-rite Roman Catholic Churches. There are also tendencies to fissiparousness even where something seemed to be being held together. The Episcopal Synod of America are traditionalists who have stayed within ECUSA (the Episcopal Church in the United States of America). Their first new bishop, coadjutor bishop-elect of Fort Worth in Texas, Jack Iker, seems likely not to get the necessary affirmation of his election by a majority of the 118 diocesan standing committees of ECUSA. The five diocesan ESA bishops (Fort Worth, Quincy, San Joaquin, Eau Clare, Fond du Lac) have written to the Presiding Bishop and the

Secretary General of the ACC to say that this is effective denial to their membership of continuing episcopal leadership and was forcing them 'to seek some form of ecclesial community which will enable us to remain true to the historic faith and practice as expressed in our Anglican heritage.'[44] The Missionary Diocese of the Americas which was set up in opposition to liberalising trends in the Anglican Church in America has severed links with ECUSA and constituted itself a new Church. Bishop A. Donald Davies, formerly Bishop of Dallas of Fort Worth and of the American Churches in Europe, said, 'It has proved impossible to live with the errors of ecclesiastical liberalism, combined with the dramatic shift that has now occurred in England's Mother Church of Anglicanism . . . . The freedom to proclaim the gospel is essential. That freedom is now ours.' This Church is to seek reunion with the 'continuing Churches' which separated from ECUSA in the 1970s and 1980s. It will dissolve its relationship with the Episcopal Synod of America, which was formed in 1989 and which established the Missionary Diocese.[45]

'In Ireland no provision was made for those clergy or laity who could not in conscience accept the Synod decision. There were no financial arrangements for the clergy. No alternative episcopal oversight was offered. Not one Church of Ireland bishop or priest resigned.'[46] But that did not hold things together. 'In September, 1990, at around the time the first women priests were ordained, a group of lay members of the Church of Ireland formed a "continuing Church"; the Church of Ireland (Traditional Rite). This body came under the episcopal oversight of the Archbishop of the Anglican Catholic Church of America, later the Anglican Church of America . . . a small Traditional Rite body has battled valiantly on, while its American parent Church split into two bodies, and two of its priests left to start their own "Evangelical Anglican Church".'[47] The tendency to split manifested itself here as in the USA. Episcopal leadership in Ireland responded to these developments by seeking to deny the ecclesiality of the new church. 'The appeals in England for charity and consideration towards those whose opinions differ contrast with the attitude of the

Bishops of the Church of Ireland, as illustrated by their statement of August, 1991... "it is not possible to enjoy with the Church of Ireland (Traditional Rite) the type of inter-Church relations which are common between most Churches today".[48]

Nowhere is this the end of the story, and we can certainly not draw any conclusions yet from this disturbance of order about the authoritativeness of a decision to ordain women taken where there is not unanimity. But we can see that a direct result of the lack of consensus is at least in the interim a disruption of common order, and that is going to challenge radically the authority to implement the decision.

We have to come back again to the fact that this was not a unanimous decision. It does not carry the authority of consensus but of majority. Nor is it the decision of the whole Church through the ages because it has been taken at a certain point in time. In itself that does not tell us whether it was right or wrong. The test of that will be more time.

That was a point made by several commentators. In the debate on the 11th November, George Carey, Archbishop of Canterbury, said, 'We have made haste slowly. That is because we want as broad a measure of unity as we can manage.'[49] Timothy Bavin, Bishop of Portsmouth, said in his heart he wanted women to be ordained, but he was not sure the Church had reached the point where it was possible to be sure it was the will of God. The Bishop of Birmingham, Mark Santer speaking later of Graham Leonard, formerly Bishop of London, suggested that 'his article in *The Catholic Herald* breathes a spirit of hustle and alarm, when what is needed is time and space for discernment'.[50]

## Conclusion: The ecclesiology

A church must be one body of Christ. Every church is a microcosm of the Church in this way. The Orthodox tradition sees it as 'the Church in each place'. Being able to meet together in worship with a pastor whom all can recognise, and above all, being able to join together in the celebration of the Eucharist, are signs of that unity. It is more than a sign; the Lord's Supper sustains the unity it signifies. If it becomes impossible for a community of Christians to come together with their Lord in this way, that community has ceased to be fully one church. It has not ceased completely to be one church. The bond of common baptism into one Lord remains. A degree of communion persists.[51]

So we have to ask what we are then left with, ecclesiologically speaking. We use the word 'church' at a number of levels below the universal, to speak of a parish as well as of a national or provincially-based ecclesial entity such as the 'Church of England'. We do not usually call a diocese 'a church'; we should, because the diocese is understood by Orthodox, Roman Catholics and Anglicans to be the fundamental unit of the Church's organisation. We have already stressed that the bishop is historically pastor of the 'local church' of his diocese, and all the parishes within it remain in his pastoral charge.

The main question to be answered, then, is what the fractured elements of the Church of England would become. In the early Church, and for most of the centuries since, an answer would be looked for in terms of one part remaining 'church', while the other would be deemed to have ceased, or partly ceased to be the Church. This is the first of three ways we can already point to, in which events which have precedents in the Church's history now look different, on today's ecumenical ecclesiological assumptions. The idea that Church must try to contain the dissidents and respect their views is something ecclesiologically new. But it is also, and crucially, different from the working principle of ecumenical dialogue, which has been that the task is not to agree to differ, but to arrive at a common faith and a shared order.

Broadly speaking, if there is a difference of opinion about a matter of faith we speak of heresy, and if a difference of opinion about a matter of order we speak of schism. Both sides in the present crisis accuse the other of making them dissenters or forcing them out of the Church. John Gummer, in his resignation letter to the synodical electors in the diocese of St. Edmundsbury and Ipswich [52] argued that 'the Church of England was claiming the right to pick and choose among those very essentials of the faith [53] of which it was the steward and never the proprietor.' ... 'By ordaining women unilaterally the Church of England no longer has the orders of the universal Church but has started its own, based not upon the authority of the Apostles but upon a two-thirds majority of the General Synod.'[54] He believes that it is the Church of England that has 'left' him, not he the Church of England. Others on both sides have felt the same. 'These people are effectively excommunicating the rest of us, refusing to accept the sacraments and jurisdiction of their bishops and threatening to set up a parallel Church'...Lack of Christian charity was also a hallmark of Donatism. The concern for financial security and the possession of church buildings and property does not go well with protestations of fidelity to the gospel spirit, but it does fit in with Donatism'.[55] Sara Lowe (St. Albans) was dismayed in the November debate to find that those who believed what the Church had always believed were called dissenters'. The ecumenical imperative is to reverse this and try to see both sides as remaining within the Church in a common order.

Secondly, the alienation across the division between those who can and those who cannot accept the ordination of women is creating alliances united perhaps only by a common view on this one point. Mark Santer speaking on Graham Leonard's proposal, Church Times, 27 November, 1992, 'My perception so far is that, among those who are dismayed and anxious, there are hardly two people who find themselves in exactly the same place.' ...'groups of unhappy Anglicans...are in danger of being united in negativity'. This taking of a 'one-issue' stand has often been a feature of division in the Church's history. But we are now under an ecumenical imperative to resist the temptation to mount such a one-plank platform. Unanimity as constitutive of ecclesial community cannot be essential except at the universal level of the Church's being, and in the context of eternity. Even there it will coexist with the diversity which reflects the variety of the gifts of the Spirit. So we certainly cannot regard solidarity either way on women priests as in itself making a local community a gathered church.

Thirdly, the process of dividing into more than one community can be seen at the level of the authority of the smallest bodies within the Church. The minimum ecclesial unit which can say yes or no to having women priests must be a pastoral unit (i.e. a parish) because it is a pastoral office which the priest normatively holds. But we have recognised that such units are not going to be unanimous, and indeed may change their minds over time. It has been suggested that the difficulty of dissident opinion in parishes which decide for or against accepting a woman priest might be solved by bussing people out regularly to another church. But that would seem to fragment local community and undermine the conception of the parish and of the diocese alike. Staying together ought to mean something more.

Nevertheless, it is natural for people to feel the need of the support of others who share their views. One commentator who has tried to live out such staying together spoke of 'those of us who hold the Catholic tradition but live and serve in parishes of a different or more general persuasion: either because we choose to worship with our local community or because there is no "Catholic" parish easily accessible.' He says that, 'unlike those who live in monolithic "catholic" parishes, we do not have the immediate comfort and support of like-minded people'.[56]

Both these tendencies, to feel excluded and to unite with others who feel the same, can easily create enemy camps, drawn up in opposition to one another. Both also create a focus inward, upon the pain and confusion from which the Church of England is suffering, and make it harder to see this break in communion in the wider context in which it affects communion between Christians worldwide. In a statement after the November vote, the Catholic Bishops of England and Wales expressed 'regret' for the Synod's decision 'first of all because it reinforces the obstacle that such ordinations place to the reconciliation of ministries which is essential to our full visible unity. Secondly we are saddened by the decision because any disunity within a particular Church makes ecumenical relations and the path to a wider unity more difficult.' Among the levels at which we should be thinking ecclesially is the higher one, at which the Church of England, and indeed the whole Anglican Communion, stands within the universal Church, and in relation to other churches.

That brings us back to the problem of what, ecclesiologically speaking, the broken pieces become, if we no longer wish to dismiss one another as 'dissidents', or to 'unchurch' one another. The model of holding a church within a church has the advantage of containing not dividing. This need not be envisaged as a circle within a circle, nor as a series of patches dotted about within the circle. Either of these pictures implies fragmentation contained, 'islanding', and indeed some of the suggestions quoted in this paper imply as much. If individuals are able to stay where they are and still feel that they belong, that is ecclesiologically much the more satisfactory outcome. The insurmountable problem is that that will bring face to face with women performing a priestly office, those who cannot accept that women can be priests, or that they can be made priests validly and efficaciously by the action of a church which is not unanimous about the possibility; and which knows that what it is doing cannot yet be accepted by all Christians everywhere. That is why difference of order is not the same as difference of faith. No ecclesiology in the Church's history has been able to accommodate radical difference over order within one church, and it is hard to see clear paths for authoritative action yet. But we must go on in faith that they will be found, because in their finding lies great ecumenical hope for the resolving of the pervasive problem of mutual recognition and reconciliation of ministry between the churches.

**Notes**

1. On impaired communion and degrees of communion in connection with the present issue, see the Eames Report which was produced by the Eames Commission after the 1988 Lambeth Conference, in accordance with Resolution 1.
2. Cf. John Habgood, *The Church Times*, 22 January, 1993.
3. Lionel E. W. Renfrey, Letter, *The Church Times*, 31 December, 1992.

4. A possibility, used by the Orthodox Churches through the ages, is to use 'economy'.

5. Sir Leslie Fielding (Chichester) voiced the view in the November debate that the legislation rested on assumptions not proven beyond reasonable doubt, and which were widely contested.

6. 'When we enter into ecumenical dialogue we take our faith as it is today. We bring our identity. But we also try to remain open to the Holy Spirit who is working for the unity of Christians, it is not for us to tell the Holy Spirit what's to be done. He should be telling us and we should be taking heed.' Cardinal Edward Cassidy, interview in *The Tablet*, 28 November, 1992.

7. Paul Vallely, *The Tablet*, 21 November, 1992.

8. John Habgood stresses the 'complex and tentative nature of the decision-making process within Anglican tradition', *The Church Times*, 22 January, 1993.

9. See *Episcopal Ministry*, Report of the Archbishops' Group on the Episcopate (1990) (The Cameron Report), Chapter 4.

10. Michael Adie, Bishop of Guildford, said in the debate that the Synod is 'representatives of the Church together searching for the truth for us today', but this qualification 'together' is important.

11. John Habgood, *The Church Times*, 22 January, 1993.

12. Debate, November 11th.

13. All churches have to be permitted to have their existence by state or nation, and in many places, as in England, the secular legislature in some way endorses the church's internal legislation.

14. That was not clearly said by all those who addressed this point in the November debate. David Silk, Archdeacon of Leicester, 'Clause 1 (1) of the measure solves at a stroke two knotty theological issues with breath- taking self assurance'. "It shall be lawful for the General Synod to make provision by canon for enabling a woman to be ordained to the office of priest".... Clause 1 (2) "Nothing in the measure shall make it lawful for a woman to be consecrated to the office of bishop". p.13 Verbatim Report of Synod Debate.

15. The Financial Provisions Measure requires clergy wishing to leave to declare that they are resigning because of the promulgation of the canon.

16. 'There was cross-party agreement in the Commons on Monday over the need to accept the General Synod's recent vote in favour of the ordination of women priests...Michael Alison, representing the Church Commissioners at Westminster, appealed to MPs to adhere to parliamentary convention when the Commons considers the issue, probably next July.' *Church Times*, 4 December, 1992.

17. He continues, 'Sometimes, only in the gravest cases, Parliament is called to protect the established Church from damaging itself irreparably. Parliament also has, in my opinion, a "legal duty of care" to ensure that bishops and priests with their laity of orthodox persuasion are given stronger safeguards than the handouts and reassurances at present offered by the Synod.' Graham A. Hodge, Letter, *Church Times*, 4 December 1992.

18. Joyce E. Dawson, *Church Times*, 20 November, 1992.

19. Stephen Trott, *Church Times*, 20 November, 1992.

20. *Church Times*, 4 December, 1992.

21. Paul Avis, *The Church Times*, 8 January, 1993. He adds, 'There is therefore no theological basis for alternative episcopal ministry in the present circumstances.... In the episcopal Churches of Sweden and Finland, bishops who do not themselves ordain women nevertheless licence them and give them pastoral support.'

22. Radio 4, The World at One, 14 January, 1993.

23. Lionel E. W. Renfrey, Letter, *Church Times*, 31 December, 1992.

24. Ken Leech, Letter, *Church Times*, 4 December, 1992.

25. *The Tablet*, 16 January, 1993.

26. See The Cameron Report chapter on suffragans.

27. 'A personal prelature, which was another model hesitantly put forward by Dr. Leonard, suffers from the problem that there is at present only one personal prelature–Opus Dei–and the function of that arrangement was to give members of the prelature some freedom from the control of local bishops. This again would be contrary to what would be sought on the English scene'. *The Tablet*, 5 December, 1992, p. 1550-1.

28. Resolution 72 of the Lambeth Conference, 1988, endorsed by bishops meeting in January 1993, i.e. that a bishop can only act as a bishop in another bishop's diocese by invitation.

29. In modern Orthodoxy, for example, Orthodox Churches in diaspora in the USA have tended to keep their sense of being 'Greek', 'Russian', and so on, and to resist forming a single Orthodox Church in the USA.

30. The use of the term 'visitor' raises an authority-question, because the Archbishops of Canterbury and York have a right of 'visitation' of the dioceses in their own provinces which allows them to enter another bishop's diocese to inspect it. The appointment of episcopal visitors will itself raise issues about who is to appoint them and on what authority. That part of the making of a bishop which involves consulting the diocese, as well as the role of the cathedral chapter, will have to be reconsidered, where there is no geographical 'see'.

31. Richard Giles, *The Tablet*, 21 November, 1992.

32. See The Cameron Report, Chapter 5.

33. See The Cameron Report.

34. *The Catholic Herald*, 20 November, 1992.

35. 'Among the objections that have been raised to the idea of a uniate Church for disaffected Anglicans is the fact that uniate Churches have been the cause of serious ill-feeling in other countries...' *The Catholic Herald*, 20 November, 1992.

36. GS 764.

37. A.J. Lane, Letter, *Church Times*, 4 December, 1992.

38. *Church Times*, 4 December, 1992.

39. *Church Times*, 13 November, 1992, p.1.

40. Verbatim Report of Synod Debate, p.46.

41. *Church Times*, 13 November, 1992, p.1.

42. Verbatim Report of Synod Debate, p.31.

43. Patricia Peacock, Letter, *Church Times*, 4 December, 1992.

44. *Church Times*, 31 December, 1992.

45. *The Tablet*, 28 November, 1992.

46. *Church Times*, 24 December, 1992, Letter from Paul Rowlandson.
47. ibid
48. ibid
49. Verbatim Report of Synod Debate, p.21.
50. *Church Times*, 27 November, 1992.
51. On degrees of communion, see the *Eames Report*.
52. *Church Times*, 11 December, 1992.
53. It is important that the issue here is one of order.
54. He continues, 'From now on nothing in creeds or orders is safe from any two-third majority that can be cobbled together.' ... 'We cannot bring up our children in partial communion with their fellow-Anglicans. We cannot train them to pass three or four churches to reach one which still proclaims orthodoxy.'
55. Gerry Reilly, Letter, *Church Times*, 31 December, 1992.
56. Brian Poulson, Letter, *Church Times*, 4 December, 1992.

# V

# Anglican 'Family Resemblance'

*Robert Hannaford*

Majority votes are not an effective way of resolving theological questions.

It will be no part of the present essay to debate the substantive question of the ordination of women to the priesthood. Many, the present author included, consider that the issue is worthy of debate and that a negative conclusion is by no means inevitable. However in this essay we shall concentrate on the question of whether or not the General Synod's decision is in keeping with the Church of England's traditional defence of the apostolic character of its sacred ministry.

There are two dangers to be avoided. On the one hand there is the temptation to try to identify a single, uniform, Anglican line of thought on this subject. On the other there is the opposite temptation of imagining that, because Anglicanism says various things under this heading, it stands for nothing in particular. The former would require a selective reading of historical Anglican texts, while the latter fails to do justice to what I shall later term the 'family resemblance' character of Anglican identity. Anglicanism cannot be said to reside exclusively in any one of its constituent traditions, but only in the dynamic interplay of them all. It is to be found neither in the lowest common denominator of these traditions nor in a fore-

shortening of the internal theological dialogue that characterises
its historical existence. Two questions will form the basis of our
enquiry. First, how far is the decision to ordain women to the
priesthood consistent with Anglican thinking on the apostolic
character of the sacred ministry? Secondly, how far can the
decision be said to be consistent with the general ethos of
Anglicanism as a family of traditions? Let us approach these
questions in reverse order.

## Defining Anglicanism

Any attempt to set theological discussion within a specifically Anglican doctrinal context is beset with problems. Unlike
the confessional churches of the Reformation or the Roman
Catholic Church, the Church of England does not possess a
clear set of foundational principles against which matters of
controversy can be measured. Recent ecumenical dialogue has
served to highlight this fact. The Roman Catholic Church, in
responding to the final ARCIC Report, asked that the agree-
ments should be supported by clearer reference to Anglican
confessional documents.[1] Paul Avis, in his book *Ecumenical
Theology*, is bold enough to suggest that there is more than a
hint of disingenuity in this request.[2] Whether or not he is
correct, it remains true that Anglicans will be hard-pressed to
furnish such documentation. The difficulty is that ecumenical dialogue has often compelled Anglicans to freeze-frame
their own internal theological dialogue. As Stephen Sykes has
pointed out, this raises the interesting question of whether or
not the ARCIC process has resulted in a 'reconfessionalization'
of Anglicanism.[3]

   In an effort to find some measure by which to identify and
assess Anglican theology authors have sometimes resorted to
terms such as 'ethos' or 'spirit', suggesting that the foundations
of Anglicanism lie more in a particular idea of Christianity than
in an established body of principles. Others in contrast have
made the bolder claim that there is a specifically Anglican

identity, although it often seems that such an identity can only be had by a selective reading of history. Paul Avis' recent book, *Anglicanism and the Christian Church*,[4] is arguably an example of such an approach. In this book Avis claims to identify a specifically Anglican ecclesiology grounded in baptism.[5] In order to arrive at his conclusion, however, first he has to exclude any consideration of evangelicalism and then rule out what he terms the 'apostolic paradigm' model of Catholic Anglican ecclesiology. This latter model, developed by the nineteenth century Tractarians, and exemplified in our own century by Michael Ramsey's important book *The Gospel and the Catholic Church*,[6] views the apostolic ministry as an essential sign of the Church's catholicity. In Avis' mind this is both inconsistent with earlier Anglicanism and too crude in its insistence upon the foundational role of apostolic order. Avis' notable contribution to Anglican scholarship is too important to be discussed in the context of a brief essay, suffice it to say that his remarks on the 'apostolic paradigm' should not go unchallenged. A definition of Anglicanism which excludes what many would regard as a legitimate expression of our tradition is unlikely to meet with universal recognition. Whether or not the Tractarians were entitled to see their theology as a legitimate expression of Anglicanism, the fact is that they did. Even if their theology is not reflected in earlier versions of Anglicanism, a view which is hard to sustain, the fact is that it has now become part of Anglican identity.

Yet others, in trying to define a specifically Anglican approach to theology, especially the theology of the church, appeal to what is described normally as classical Anglicanism. Attention is focussed upon a broad sweep of seventeenth century theologians whose work is held up as the epitome of Anglicanism. Their work is said to provide concrete evidence of a specifically Anglican approach to theology and spirituality. They are said to reflect the Anglican representation of a Reformed Catholicism at its best. This approach was particularly popular amongst the Tractarians, who were at some pains to support the claim that their recognition of the catholicity of the Church of England was reflected in the work of earlier Anglican theologians. We have their quest for a classical Anglican position to thank for the publication in the nineteenth century of the *Library of Anglo-Catholic Theology*. This important historical resource, containing the theological works of many significant High Church Anglican theologians, represents a serious attempt to recapture the past in the cause of the Catholic revival.

The popularity of this approach was given added impetus by the publication in 1935 of *Anglicanism: The Thought and Practice of the Church of England, Illustrated from the Religious Literature of the Seventeenth Century*. This book, which was compiled and edited by Paul Elmer More and Frank Leslie Cross, contains extracts covering the period from 1594, the date of the publication of the first four books of Richard Hooker's *Ecclesiastical Polity*, to 1691, a date roughly coinciding with the beginnings of the Non-Juring movement.[7]

This approach to Anglican identity has much to commend it. Theologians such as Richard Hooker and Joseph Hall, whose work exemplifies this enormously creative period in the history of Anglican thinking, are arguably the best and most creative minds ever produced by the Church of England. However, the fact remains that their theology is classic and not foundational. While a classic text might carry great authority, it does not in the end bind subsequent generations. Classical Anglicanism may provide us with leading examples of the Anglican way of doing theology but it does not provide us with anything like a foundational core. The English Reformation did not produce a single theologian to whom appeal can be made in settling disputes. Indeed Anglican apologists of the age in question could even boast, as did Chillingworth, that we 'call no man master on the earth.'[8]

There are significant problems associated with the appeal to a classical version of Anglicanism. A careful examination of the theologians of this period soon reveals considerable diversity of opinion. Furthermore the theologians usually referred to, do not in themselves constitute anything like an exhaustive cross section of English Christianity in the seventeenth century. While there is perhaps a degree of wishful thinking in L.S.Thornton's description of Richard Hooker as 'the father of Anglo- Catholic Theology', the theologians quoted in More and Cross do in the main represent a reformed catholicism.[9] Such a selection obviously excludes those on the puritan wing of English Christianity. Finally one must note that seventeenth century ecclesiology, with its undoubted dependence upon erastianism, would be very uncongenial to contemporary Catholic Anglicans.

## Anglican Family Resemblance

It is perhaps more helpful to think of Anglican Identity, as John Macquarrie does, in terms of family resemblance. Macquarrie uses the term when dealing with a representative group of Anglican theologians.[10] I would like to use the term in a much more general sense. We have seen how difficult it is to assess the Anglican approach to doctrinal matters. Our inability to point to anything like a clear set of foundational doctrinal principles causes much frustration amongst our ecumenical interlocutors. And yet Anglicanism does accept certain norms and standards of authority. Our liturgy and historic formularies make frequent reference to the supreme authority of the Holy Scriptures and to the interpretative significance of the Catholic Creeds. Anglicans are also in the main ready to accept the authority of the Ecumenical Councils, differing slightly over whether this extends to four or six. However, what we do not possess are definitive and binding interpretations of these various elements of general authority. Instead Anglicanism has a number of different traditions, each claiming authority for its reading of Anglican doctrinal and liturgical formularies. It is part of the peculiar genius of Anglicanism to have nurtured from common historical roots, paths of theology and spirituality which normally serve to identify separate ecclesial groups. Catholics, Evangelicals and liberals, all alike lay their claim to Anglicanism. This means that Anglicanism cannot be found exclusively in any one of its component traditions, nor in a sort of lowest common denominator of all of them.

Describing Anglican doctrinal identity in terms of family resemblance involves an acknowledgement of its complexity. Family resemblance is characterised by a series of overlapping similarities and relationships and not by a single idea shared by all. It is an identity of proportionality rather than one of collective conformity. Instead of looking for a single common denominator one should look instead for a series of beliefs and practices. Some of these may overlap and complement one another, but others seem to have little or nothing in common. Such is the nature of families, where distant relatives often seem to have more in common with members of other families.

As members of a family Anglicans acknowledge a common sacramental lineage in baptism and episcopal confirmation. They share family table fellowship in the Eucharist and are sufficiently confident in the strength of their ties to invite others, from outside their immediate family, to share in this. Furthermore, they are ready to acknowledge that not just anything will count as acceptable behaviour and belief in their family, but within these limits they are tolerant. In articulating these parameters they can point to the beliefs expressed in their liturgies and in the official and semi-official documents of their communion. Nonetheless a considerable degree of freedom is allowed to people in interpreting this tradition. Indeed, when asked to specify precisely what this tradition is Anglicans generally have to agree to disagree amongst themselves.

Should this be regarded as a fatal weakness in a church? It is not immediately obvious that it should. Family resemblance is a form of identity, but it is not one founded upon uniformity of belief or practice. The philosopher Ludwig Wittgenstein used the expression 'family resemblance' in his anti-essentialist analysis of language. He argued that just because language is a single category this should not lead us into supposing that meaning can be reduced to a single essential thing. Language, he claimed, is characterised not by a single common feature but by a series of relationships. I do not want to press this comparison too far but it does illustrate the usefulness of this particular model of identity. It identifies things in terms of a series of overlapping relationships without insisting upon one single thing being shared by every member of the family.

This seems to me to be an apt description of Anglican identity. Anglicans are not united by a single confessional core, but there are undoubtedly varying shades of resemblance to be found both within and between its different strands of churchmanship.

While it does not make use of the expression 'family resemblance' the report of the Archbishops' Commission on Doctrine published in 1938 seems to echo this approach. The Commission, which was set up in 1922, had as its brief: 'To consider the nature and grounds of Christian doctrine with a view to demonstrating the extent of existing agreement within the Church of England and with a view to investigating how far it is possible to remove or diminish existing differences.'[11] It is a particularly striking feature of the report that, apart from a brief three page discussion of the Articles of Religion, nowhere does it make mention of specifically Anglican doctrinal positions. In defending this the report offers what has become a characteristically Anglican explanation but also hints at an additional reason which reflects our own analysis. In the Introduction we read:

> There are systems of Catholic Theology and of Protestant Theology. To them we have, of course, owed much. But there is not, and the majority of us do not desire that there should be, a system of distinctively Anglican Theology. The Anglican Churches have received and hold the faith of Catholic Christendom, but they have exhibited a rich variety in methods of approach and interpretation.[12]

This is the bold claim, sometimes made by Anglicans, that they hold no doctrines peculiar to themselves but only the faith of the one Church of Christ. Bishop Hensley Henson once put the position thus: if a doctrine is true, the Church of England believes it. The words quoted above also hint at another, rather different explanation, namely that Anglicanism by its very nature cannot avoid speaking with a number of different voices. The Introduction continues by saying of the Anglican Churches that

> They are the heirs of the Reformation as well as of Catholic tradition; and they hold together in a single fellowship of worship and witness those whose chief attachment is to each of these, and also those whose attitude to the distinctively Christian tradition is most deeply affected by the tradition of a free and liberal culture which is historically the bequest of the Greek spirit and was recovered for Western Europe at the Renaissance.[13]

It is important to note here the frank acknowledgment that many Anglicans see their chief attachment as being to theological traditions which are not specifically Anglican. The compilers of the report adopt this as something like a procedural principle. They resist any attempt to cut short the dialogue between these different traditions, preferring instead to set them alongside one another: 'Our aim...is not specifically to commend the doctrine of the Church, but to examine the differences of interpretation current in the Church of England and to elucidate the relations of these one to another.'[14] Anglicanism does not reside in a synthesis of its component traditions for this could not 'have the variety and richness characteristic of the traditions themselves.'[15] It is rather to be found in the juxtaposition and interplay of its family of traditions.

Family resemblance as a form of identity is both strong and fragile at the same time. It is strong because it can incorporate diversity but it is fragile insofar as it depends upon a willingness to go beyond mere toleration in sanctioning texts and policies which permit variant theological readings. This last point has a very direct bearing upon our topic so it will be worth spending a little time on it.

Toleration implies a willingness to respect the views of others. Anglicans can lay no special claim to this virtue, but Anglican identity depends upon something that goes much deeper. Where the identity of family resemblance is concerned it is not enough merely to accommodate those with whom one disagrees; each member of the family must be in a position to authenticate their interpretation of the tradition. That is to say, all shades of churchmanship must be able to lay equal claim to their reading of the historic Anglican formularies. Catholics, Evangelicals and Liberals alike must be able to point to public features of Anglicanism, such as the liturgy and canons, in support of their interpretation of the tradition. All traditions must in a sense be able to claim Anglicanism as their own. Anything which challenges this calls into question the nature of Anglican identity.

When one tradition can no longer sincerely claim that its beliefs are enshrined in the public face of Anglicanism this means that it has effectively been excluded from the family. It can no longer claim with integrity that its views overlap with the other traditions or that they coincide with the established public practice of the Anglican Church. This is precisely the situation in which many Catholic Anglicans now find themselves. Up to this point in history they have been able to secure their position within the Church of England by pointing to elements within its collective life which support their own self identity as Anglicans. Many now find their whole reading of the Anglican doctrine of the apostolic nature of the ministry called into question. Whereas in the past they have been able to appeal sincerely to the Ordinal and to the practice of the Church of England in support of their claim that their church has retained the ancient catholic and apostolic ministry of bishop, priest and deacon, they now find that appeal to ancient practice called into question.

We must then face up to the genuine possibility that by its action the General Synod has called into doubt the identity of Anglicanism as a family of traditions. This decision may make it quite impossible for substantial numbers of Catholic Anglicans to feel that their reading of Christianity is any longer represented in the new version of Anglicanism that now exists. This is undoubtedly a new and quite unparalleled development in the life of the Church of England. For the first time since the Reformation one of its constituent traditions faces the painful possibility that its reading of Anglican formularies may no longer be supportable.

In a helpful and pastorally sensitive letter to *The Independent* Bishop Gavin Reid, himself a supporter of women's ordination to the priesthood, stated that both sides in this debate must be respected.[16] Both must be able to lay equal claim to represent authentic Anglicanism. This is the challenge now facing the Church of England, to produce structures which allow Catholic Anglicans to maintain, with integrity, that their way of being Anglicans remains a legitimate interpretation within the overall family of traditions.

## An Anglican Reading of the Apostolic Character of the Priesthood

We have ruled out already any consideration of the merits of the case for and against the principle of women's ordination to the priesthood. Some have opposed this development on the grounds of a particular theological anthropology, arguing that the sexes are complementary in nature, and that there is something intrinsically incompatible in a woman assuming a role of sacramental headship in the church. Others have claimed that the maleness of Christ makes it impossible for women to symbolize the priesthood of Christ. Since neither case is clearly and unambiguously formed in scripture or the tradition of the church they cannot be taken as conclusive. More decisive is the appeal to the unchanging witness of Catholic practice; there can be no gainsaying that the admission of women to the priesthood is a very recent invention. However, as we shall see at a later point, even this does not in itself rule out the possibility that such a development could and should occur. What grounds there could be for departing from this uniform practice are as yet unclear. Certainly the current debate within Anglicanism has not yet achieved anything like a genuine consensus on this matter.

In the previous section we raised the question of whether or not Catholic Anglicans any longer can lay claim to find their faith represented in the public face of Anglicanism. What raises this is not the ordination of women as such, but the apparent abandonment by the Church of England of the idea that historical continuity is an essential feature of a properly apostolic form of ministry. It is not the admission of women to the priesthood that in itself constitutes the problem, it is the decision of the Church of England to depart from its, hitherto unquestioned, acceptance of the normative authority of universal catholic practice.

As our reflections on the nature of Anglican identity have made clear, it is extremely difficult to identify a single definitive Anglican position on matters to do with Christian doctrine. Indeed we have been forced to conclude that Anglicanism is best understood as a family of traditions. Therefore it would be wrong for me to claim that what follows represents anything like an official or semi-official Anglican dogma. However, the position outlined below can lay claim to represent a key strand in Anglican thinking on the sacred ministry. While it may not be the only Anglican theological position on this matter, it is one that has exerted an enormous, and indeed decisive, influence on the public policy of the Church of England and Anglicanism in general. Indeed, it has at times been so influential as to amount to the nearest thing to a binding feature of Anglicanism.

The Ordinal, normally bound in one volume with the *Book of Common Prayer*, is generally taken as one of the nearest things that the Church of England possesses to a foundational document. In the Preface we find the following explanation of the Church of England's attitude towards the foundations of the sacred ministry:

> It is evident unto all men diligently reading Holy Scripture and ancient Authors, that from the Apostle's time there have been these Orders of Ministers in Christ's Church; Bishops, Priests, and Deacons. Which offices were evermore had in such reverend estimation, that no man might

presume to execute any of them, except he were first called, tried, examined, and known to have such qualities as are requisite for the same; and also by publick Prayer, with Imposition of Hands, were approved and admitted thereunto by lawful authority. And therefore, to the intent that these Orders may be continued, and reverently used and esteemed, in the Church of England; No man shall be accounted or taken to be a lawful Bishop, Priest, or Deacon in the Church of England, or suffered to execute any of the said functions, except he be called, tried, examined, and admitted thereunto, according to the form hereafter following, or hath had formerly Episcopal Consecration or Ordination.

Here we have an unambiguous declaration that the Church of England conceives its Orders of Ministry to be a continuation of apostolic practice. There are two features to note in particular. First, this statement of intention establishes the principle that in relation to the question of holy orders historical continuity is vital. Indeed, it is implied that it is the witness of the historic practice of Christ's Church that alone lends authority to the continuation of this form of ordained ministry. Secondly, the wording clearly indicates that the appeal is not simply to the Apostles but to the practice of the Church at all times. In other words, here in the Ordinal we have a clear example of what Lynne Leeder, in her article in this book, has referred to as the appeal to the Great Church. The Church of England intends to retain the historic ministry, and locates its authority for doing so in the unchanging witness of the Church throughout the ages.

This interpretation is reflected in the reply of the Archbishops of Canterbury and York to the Bull of Pope Leo XIII *Apostolicae Curae* condemning Anglican orders. In this document, usually known as *Saepius Officio*, the Archbishops address 'All the Bishops of the Catholic Church'. They write concerning Anglican Orders in terms which clearly imply that the Church of England is at one with the Roman Church in wishing to retain the historic apostolic ministry. Their case is built up by a series of arguments which set Anglican practice against the background of the historic tradition which, it is claimed, the Church of England shares with the Roman Catholic Church. What is clear, at least from the Anglican side, is that the two Archbishops understand the Church of England to be ordaining men to a form of ministry which Rome should recognise as comparable in form and derivation to its own. As they put it: 'The intention of our Fathers was to keep and continue these offices which come down from earliest times, and "reverently to use and esteem them," in the sense, of course, in which they were received from the Apostles and had been up to that time in use.'[17]

It is important to realise that this Anglican appeal to apostolic practice in defence of its ministry is not simply an appeal to antiquity. It is, above all, a declaration that in ordination the Church of England understands itself to be doing what the rest of Catholic Christendom does. In other words, it is an appeal to an authority that is greater than Anglicanism itself. The recent Board of Mission and Unity report, *The Priesthood of the Ordained Ministry*, describes the Church's ministry of bishops, priests and deacons as ultimately an aspect of 'the tradition it has received from the Church of the apostles'.[18] Moreover the report also insists that this same ministry is something which the Church of England has received from the 'Universal Church'.[19] It also repeats a constantly reiterated Anglican claim that those ordained to its ministry are in fact ordained as 'bishops or presbyters of the whole church.'[20]

As well as insisting upon the universal character of the ordained ministry the report also suggests that there is a link between this and 'the universality or catholicity of the church'.[21] How far Anglicanism has ever been committed to the view that the apostolic ministry is part of the *esse* of the church is a matter of some dispute. Anglican theologians can be produced to support both sides of the case. For historical reasons the debate on this matter has tended to focus on episcopacy. This is understandable given the situation facing the Church of England in the sixteenth and seventeenth centuries. At this time

Anglicanism was defending its position against Rome on the one hand and radical protestantism on the other.

Many Anglican theologians showed a very natural reticence in approaching this issue. While wishing to defend their form of ministry they did not want to give offence to other non-episcopal reformed churches. Richard Hooker is a case in point. As Paul Avis has pointed out, Hooker drew a distinction between mutable and immutable positive divine law,[22] and placed episcopacy firmly in the former category; such things, Hooker claimed, can be changed according to circumstances.

> Laws which the church from the beginning universally hath observed were some delivered by Christ himself, with a charge to keep them to the world's end, as the law of baptizing and administering the holy eucharist; some brought in afterwards by the apostles, yet not without the special direction of the Holy Ghost, as occasions did arise.[23]

This means, according to Hooker, that the church 'hath power to alter, with general consent and upon necessary occasions, even the positive law of the apostles, if there be no command to the contrary, and it manifestly appears to her that change of times have clearly taken away the very reasons of God's first institution.'[24] Nonetheless we must be cautious in interpreting Hooker. His position on this, as on so many questions, is a complex one. As Beatrice M Hamilton Thompson pointed out in her contribution to *The Apostolic Ministry*, a collection of essays by Catholic Anglican scholars published in 1946, there are contradictions in Hooker's writings, indicating his inveterate habit of modifying his position as he wrote.[25] His views, quoted above, from Book VII of *Of The Laws of Ecclesiastical Polity*, must be interpreted in the light of his opinion expressed further on in Book VII: 'Let us not fear to be herein bold and peremptory, that if anything in the Church's government, surely the first institution of bishops was from heaven, was even of God, the Holy Ghost was the author of it.'[26]

Whatever we make of Hooker's own position on this matter, he was undoubtedly claimed by later advocates of the doctrine of the divine right of Bishops as an influential upholder of their views.

Before passing on we should note that Hooker also advanced a view of the authority of the apostolic ministry which anticipates the problems thrown up by modern biblical and historical scholarship. Modern scholarship has made it increasingly difficult to hold to a rigidly historical interpretation of the apostolic succession. The problem with this, of course, is the impossibility of identifying any one definitive model of ministry in apostolic and early post-apostolic times. To those who want to insist that the threefold ministry of bishops, priests, and deacons is derived directly from the actions of the apostles themselves, this poses a problem. While Hooker was prepared to entertain the idea that this order was of apostolic origin, he did not think that its divine authority need rest upon this. Whether the apostles actually instituted episcopacy is for him a secondary consideration since it 'had either divine appointment beforehand, or divine approbation afterwards, and is in that respect to be acknowledged the ordinance of God.'[27] Hooker's position anticipates the now much more common Anglican view that it is the universal practice of the Church rather than strict apostolic derivation that validates this form of ministry.

Although all Anglican theologians in the sixteenth century consider it important to defend the historic apostolic ministry some are prepared to concede that it belongs to 'ceremonies or rites' that National Churches are at liberty to modify.[28] However, Henry Chadwick points out that from the 1590's Anglicans adopted a harder position, claiming that the episcopate in particular is a gift of God which no particular Church is at liberty to change.[29] Increasingly the historic ministry was seen as a keystone in the life of the Church, a guarantee of her sacramental continuity.

While it would be right to say, as Richard A. Norris does, that the Anglican Church has never unambiguously held that the apostolic ministry belongs to the *esse* of the Church [ie. to the very definition of the Church], it remains true that in her public actions and declarations she has generally behaved as though it does.[30] The famous 'Chicago-Lambeth Quadrilateral', for example, includes Catholic order in the list of factors essential to 'the visible unity of the church'. Too many recent ecumenical ventures have failed because of Anglican insistence upon episcopacy for us not to conclude that, at least from a practical point of view, Anglicanism regards Catholic order as having a direct bearing upon the visible identity or being of the Church.

What emerges from our discussion so far is the extent to which Anglicanism has sought to ground the authority for its ordained ministry in an appeal to the practice of the Universal Church. While this appeal has often involved a reference to the practice of the early Church and the teaching of the Fathers, it has also included acknowledgment of the living tradition which Anglicanism shares with other Catholic churches. In other words the Anglican Church has always believed itself to have quite consciously retained a form of ordained ministry which it claims to share with the rest of Catholic Christianity.

What price now the appeal to catholic and apostolic practice? The decision of the General Synod to admit women to the priesthood poses a serious threat to this particular tradition of Anglicanism. Anglicans cannot point to the practice of the Universal Church in defence of either their decision or the new form of ministry created by it. It is simply impossible to avoid the conclusion that for the first time the Church of England, in making changes to apostolic order, is doing a thing of its own invention. There is absolutely no defence possible on grounds of the practice which the Church of England has hitherto claimed to share with the rest of the Universal Church. The problem is not the ordination of women as such but the fact that Anglicans may no longer be able to point to universal Catholic practice in defence of their form of ministry.

It is this problem that particularly exercises Catholic Anglicans. Many who remain agnostic on the principle of women's ordination to the priesthood will find it difficult to avoid reaching the conclusion that their Church has decisively shifted the locus of authority for its ordained ministry. Since there is no precedent outside Anglicanism for such a change, they will be forced to conclude that the firm foundation of historic Catholic practice has been exchanged for something less substantial.

It has been said by some that the decision to admit women to the priesthood does not change the institution itself or our understanding of it, but simply opens it up to a larger constituency. The claim is that the basic ontological structure of the priesthood is not affected by this decision. This is an important question and one must tread carefully in addressing it. Stating that the decision to ordain women to the priesthood *would* affect its ontological structure implies that it would be impossible ever to conceive of such a move. Only those willing to state that women should never be admitted to the priesthood could ever hold such a strong view. Many who currently oppose what the Church of England is planning to do would not go so far. However, even while one might be prepared to acknowledge that the admission of women would have a neutral affect on the basic ontological structure of the priesthood, this is not in itself an end of the matter.

It is by no means inconceivable that the whole Church could decide to admit women to the priesthood. Undoubtedly many would resist such a move, but they would have no fundamental grounds for doing so. The universal Church possesses the right, and indeed the duty, to interpret historic tradition. Given such a scenario, it would be clear that in ordaining women the Church was intending to develop and not change its tradition. Since women would be admitted to a priesthood acknowledged by the whole Church, no fundamental change would be made to the order itself. Its authority would continue to reside in the practice of the universal Church.

It is one thing to acknowledge that the Universal Church could, under the guidance of the Holy Spirit, decide to admit women to the priesthood. It is quite another to suggest that the Church of England can and should act unilaterally in this matter. The difficulty with such an act lies precisely in its apparent abandonment of the grounds upon which Anglicanism has traditionally justified its retention of the historic ministry. In abrogating to itself the right to make such a fundamental change the Church of England has denominationalized its sacred ministry. It has exchanged the appeal to the witness of the Universal Church for a narrower appeal to Anglican self-judgment. The basic ontological structure of the priesthood might remain unchanged but its authority would be severely impaired.

## The Ordination of Women: A Scenario for a Change

Having suggested that the admission of women to the priesthood need not be incompatible with Catholic tradition, it now falls to us to examine the conditions under which such a development might be conceivable. How, then, might such a change be possible without, at the same time, undermining the apostolic character of the historic ministry?

First, a change would be legitimate if it could be demonstrated, beyond reasonable doubt, that it was never the intention of the Church explicitly to exclude women from the priesthood. Many accepted the decision of the Church of England to admit women to the diaconate because there is clear historical precedence for this. Women were admitted to this, or a like order, in the early church, and the contemporary church is therefore simply restoring something that has been lost. No such defence can be advanced in the case of the priesthood. There is simply no historical evidence to indicate that the Church did not intend to exclude women from this order. The unwavering practice of not ordaining women to the priesthood constitutes a weighty, if silent, barrier even for those of us who are willing to accept that the time is ripe for a re-examination of traditional Christian thinking about gender and human identity.

Secondly, change could be envisaged if it can be shown that the exclusion of women from the priesthood was clearly dependent upon social and cultural factors that no longer apply, such as a belief in the inferiority of women. Karl Rahner adopted this position in his criticism of the 1976 Vatican Declaration *Inter*

*Insigniores*, which argued that the Church cannot abandon the pattern established by Christ of only calling male Apostles. Rahner finds this case not proven:

> The conclusion seems inescapable that the attitude of Jesus and his Apostles is sufficiently explained by the cultural and sociological milieu in which they acted and had to act . . . It does not seem to be proved that the actual behaviour of Jesus and the Apostles implies a norm of divine revelation in the strict sense of the term.[31]

As John McDade points out, commenting on Rahner's argument, the claim that the Church's uniform practice has a binding force for all time overlooks the fact that the Church 'has never seriously addressed the matter in a discussion which did not feel the distorting impact of classical misogyny'.[32] The time is now ripe, he suggests, for a serious and considered discussion of this whole question.

In order to demonstrate such a case it would have to be shown both that the factors leading to the exclusion of women from the priesthood were largely or exclusively social and cultural, and that these conditions have no direct bearing upon divine revelation. That is, it would have to be shown that cultural ideas, ultimately unrelated to the Christian message itself, contributed directly to the exclusion of women from the ministerial priesthood and the episcopate. The case would be made even stronger, of course, if it can be demonstrated that the factors leading to the exclusion of women are ultimately inconsistent with foundational Christian truth.

If alien ideas about women can be shown to have played a part, then this could be used to demonstrate either that changing social and cultural conditions render the exclusion unnecessary or that change would serve to correct Christian practice in the light of a greater truth. While many would now be prepared to admit that Christian theology and spirituality have been distorted by patriarchal and hierarchical conceptions of human nature, there are still a number of considerations to be born in mind before moving in the direction of change.

Even though many are growing ever more convinced by the feminist analysis of Christian history and theology, this does not in itself constitute anything like a decisive reason for overturning the uniform practice of Catholic Christianity. If, as many suspect, contingent cultural conditions played a decisive role in the exclusion of women from the priesthood we would need to be convinced that the case for their inclusion was not for its part largely dependant upon a change in secular culture. In other words, it would have to be shown that the grounds for change lay unambiguously in an authentic re-interpretation of those elements of Christian theology that led to the exclusion of women from the priesthood in the first place. That this would be a mammoth task no one can doubt, and yet the seriousness of the issue demands that nothing less will suffice. The tragedy is that the task is still in its infancy and many members of the Church of England can see no good reason for departing from existing practice.

How might such a change be brought about without seriously threatening the unity of the Church? As we have suggested, it would have to rest upon a clear foundation of theological truth. Moreover, this would have to be decisive enough to offset the witness of traditional practice. Anything less would result in the situation in which we now find ourselves, with many doubting the apostolicity of a priesthood open to women. It might be objected that the debate on the ordination of women has been going on for at least twenty years in the Church of England. The difficulty is that the surface of this issue has barely been scratched. In addition no serious attempt has been made to engage other churches, sharing our pattern of ordained ministry, in discussion on this issue. Certainly the Church of England has not heeded the fraternal advice offered by the Roman Catholic and Orthodox Churches on this matter.

Given the fractured nature of the Church, insisting that a General Council is the only appropriate body to authorise such a change sounds suspiciously like another way of ensuring that it could never happen. However, when fundamental matters of faith and order are at issue the Church is wise to respect the convention that nothing less than a General Council is needed to test the matter. Such a council would ensure that the national concerns of a particular church are tested against the wider concerns of the universal body of believers. Within such a context the distinction between what is of only momentary value can be sifted from what is likely to be of lasting significance. It is unfair to insist that the question of the ordination of women must await the re-union of Christendom and the calling of a genuinely ecumenical council. No Church could carry out its mission if fundamental decisions had to await the settling of all theological issues currently dividing the Catholic Church. In the interim, however, the very least that should be expected is an observation of the important principle that in fundamental matters of faith and order national churches or synods should not act unilaterally. This is not to say that the lone prophetic voice is always wrong. Church history reminds us that national churches and even individual Christians sometimes speak with greater authority than the wider councils of the Church. The point is, surely, that action taken in the absence of a genuine consensus amongst the faithful is a threat to the unity of the Church.

It might be objected that in deciding to act in the way that it has the Church of England is acting in a way that is consistent with a growing consensus within the world-wide Anglican communion. How far this is actually true remains to be seen. Far more disturbing about such a claim, however, is the way in which it appears to denominationalize the appeal to the practice of the Universal Church. As we have seen in matters to do with Church order the Church of England has traditionally appealed to the practice of the Great Church in defence of its own polity. The Church of England now finds itself in a position where it can no longer appeal to a witness that is wider than those churches currently in communion with the Archbishop of Canterbury. In this respect at least it has cut itself off from the rest of the Catholic Church.

**Notes**

1. See J.Ratzinger, 'Anglican-Catholic Dialogue–Its Problems and Hopes', *Insight*, 1, pp.2-11, 1983, and *Observations on the Final Report of ARCIC*, Sacred Congregation for the Doctrine of the Faith, 1981.
2. London, 1986
3. 'ARCIC and the Papacy: An Examination of the Documents on Authority', *The Modern Churchman*, 25, 1982, pp.9-18.
4. Edinburgh, 1989.
5. Ibid.p.304.
6. London, 1936.
7. London, 1935.
8. Chillingworth quoted in More & Cross
9. *Richard Hooker*, London, 1924, p.101.
10. 'The Anglican Theological Tradition' in *The Anglican Tradition*, Ed. Richard Holloway, London, 1984, p.29.
11. *Doctrine in the Church of England*, London, 1938, 'Introduction', p.19.
12. Ibid. p.25.
13. Ibid.
14. Ibid. p.6f.
15. Ibid. p.7.
16. *The Independent*, 19 January, 1993.
17. *Saepius Officio*, p.28 in the Church Literature Association edition, 1977.
18. London, 1986, p.102.
19. Ibid.
20. Ibid, p. 101.
21. Ibid.
22. P. Avis. op.cit.. 1989. p.57f.
23. *Of the Laws of Ecclesiastical Polity,* Book VII Ch. v.8
24. ibid
25. 'The Post-Reformation Episcopate in England' in *The Apostolic Ministry*, Ed. K.E. Kirk, London, 1946, p.428.
26. *Of the Laws of Ecclesiastical Polity,* Book VII Ch. v.10
27. *Of the Laws of Ecclesiastical Polity,* Book VII Ch. v.2
28. See Article XXXIV, 'Of the Traditions of the Church'.
29. 'Tradition, Fathers and Councils' in *The Study of Anglicanism*, Ed. Stephen Sykes and John Booty, London, 1988, p.102.
30. 'Episcopacy' in Sykes & Booty, Ibid., p.306.
31. 'Women and the Priesthood', *Theological Investigations*, London, 1961, Vol. 20. pp.35-47.
32. John McDade, 'The Ministries of Women', *The Month*, December 1992, pp. 458-460.

# VI

# Sacramental Life and Impaired Communion

A dialogue between the Revd. Michael Watts and Father
Edward Yarnold, S.J.

**Watts:** How is communion established?

**Yarnold:** ARCIC II gave an answer to this question in its
statement *Church as Communion*. The answer given there is
that communion means 'sharing in the divine life, being united
with the Father, through his Son, in the Holy Spirit, and
consequently to be in fellowship with all those who share in the
same gift of eternal life'. Within a local community, its communion means that it is 'a gathering of the baptised brought
together by the apostolic preaching, confessing the one faith,
celebrating the one eucharist, and led by an apostolic ministry'.
For such local churches to be in communion among themselves,
'it is required that all the essential constitutive elements of
ecclesial communion are present and mutually recognised in
each of them' (n.43).

The Commission proceeded to set out a list of these constitutive elements of communion. 'It is rooted in the confession of
the one apostolic faith, revealed in the Scriptures, and set forth
in the Creeds. It is founded upon one baptism. The one
celebration of the eucharist is its pre-eminent expression and
focus.' This communion is expressed in shared commitment to

mission, mutual concern, acceptance of the same fundamental moral values and the same hope of the coming of God's Kingdom. Both local and universal communion require also a common ministry of oversight, which involves 'shepherding, teaching and the celebration of the sacraments, especially the eucharist'. Within this ministry, which has 'both collegial and primatial dimensions', 'the episcopal ministry of a universal primate finds its role as the visible focus of unity' (n.46).

**Watts:** What impairs communion?

**Yarnold:** The Vatican II decree on Ecumenism recognises that communion admits of degrees: 'those who believe in Christ and have been properly baptized are put in some kind of communion with the Catholic church (*in quadam cum ecclesia catholica communione*), even though this communion is imperfect' (n.3). In the same spirit Pope John Paul II and Archbishop Robert Runcie in their Common Declaration of 2 October 1989 spoke of 'that certain yet imperfect communion we already share' (quoted in ARCIC II, *Church as Communion*, n.51).

The presupposition here is that the churches in the twentieth century are not responsible for their present separation. The term 'impaired communion' on the other hand implies that the present generation has been responsible for diminishing the communion that used to exist among them, so that what was full communion of the kind described in the first answer above has now become imperfect. It is a term which has been applied to the consequences of the decision of many Anglican provinces to ordain women to the priesthood. This decision has meant that the Anglican Communion now contains people who cannot recognise the ministry of all those who have been regularly ordained according to the canonical rules, and therefore in conscience cannot receive the eucharist with fellow Anglicans at the hands of such a minister. The Anglican communion is therefore a 'communion' of people who cannot all receive holy communion together. The same might be true in the Roman Catholic Church of people who felt they could not receive holy communion from a priest or together with laypeople who gave support to exploiters of the poor.

**Watts:** This inability to recognise the ordination of women raises the question of the validity of orders. What does validity mean?

**Yarnold:** With ordinations, as indeed with all sacraments, one must distinguish validity from regularity (sometimes called liceity). Ordinations are regular if they have been conferred according to the canonical rules; they are valid if they are what they claim to be.

This distinction needs further explanation. It presupposes that, although some irregularities in the conferring of orders are not serious enough to nullify the effect of the ordination, others may be. Let us consider some possible cases. A bishop, perhaps because he was acting in secret at a time of persecution, might not be wearing the correct attire when ordaining a priest; such an irregularity would not however have the result that the person so ordained was not a priest at all. Again a bishop might perform an ordination outside his diocese without the permission of the relevant bishop; in this case again the irregularity would not be considered to reduce the ordination to an empty form which would leave the 'ordained' person no more than a layman. On the other hand one can easily envisage cases in which the attempted ordination would completely fail to produce the desired effect of making a priest, or in other words would be invalid. This would be so if the person ordaining had not the power to ordain (being for example a layman), or if the ordination were simply a scene in a play, or if the rite employed was incapable of expressing the making of a priest (as in the mythical ordination of Matthew Parker to be Archbishop of Canterbury at the Nag's Head tavern in 1559 by the placing of the Bible on his neck with the words: 'Take thou authority to preach the word of God sincerely').

Consequently validity or invalidity is a matter of objective fact. To put the defect right the church cannot just 'recognise' the orders as valid, because you cannot recognise what is not there. If the orders are invalid the church must do something to *make* them valid; a new form of ordination must be correctly celebrated.

The question whether women can be ordained to the priesthood would be not too difficult to solve if it were simply a matter of the regularity or irregularity of such an act. All that would be needed would be a change in canon law to permit such ordinations. But the question is rather if, when a bishop goes through the form of ordaining a woman according to canon law, such a woman will be a priest at all. The ordination of a horse or a resisting captive would be invalid, because the subject must be a free human being; no change in canon law would make the action valid. Is the same true of the ordination of a woman, because the subject must be male? That is the heart of the dispute.

It is important to draw a further distinction, namely that between the validity and the fruitfulness of a sacrament. The fact that there are unmistakable signs that the ministry of a priest has helped Christians to faith and holiness of life is not sure evidence of the validity of that priest's orders. Although the church is obliged to make sure that sacraments are validly conferred, God is under no such limitations. The Spirit blows where he wills (Jn 3.8); he is free to give his grace where he chooses, even in response to the ministries of an invalidly ordained priest.

This last point can be expressed in terms of the traditional distinction between the two levels at which a sacrament is effective. The ultimate effect of a sacrament (known as its 'reality', or in Latin *res*) is the grace which it confers on the recipient. However there is also an intermediate effect, namely the new or deeper relationship with the Church which the sacrament brings about, and which in turn is the cause of the 'reality' of the grace which is received. Thus at baptism the new Christian is incorporated into Christ's body, the Church, and as a result receives the indwelling of the Holy Spirit as the source of sanctifying grace; so too at ordination the new priest is first established in his priestly position in the Church, and as a result receives the promise that the Holy Spirit will give him the grace he needs for his new calling. This intermediary ecclesial effect became known as the *res et sacramentum*, as it is both a reality conferred by the sacrament and the sign and guarantee of the grace given to the person in fulfilment of their new calling.[1] To apply these terms to the distinction between validity and fruitfulness, one would say that the fruitfulness concerns the *res*, but validity concerns the *res et sacramentum*; God is free to use a minister as a means of grace even if he does not possess the ecclesial reality of priesthood.

I must however acknowledge that not all Roman Catholic theologians today subscribe to the understanding of validity I have been expounding, though it could fairly be described as the "official" view. John Coventry, for example, puts forward the alternative view that a valid sacrament is one which is 'de facto recognised or guaranteed by the Church as a true sacrament'; a sacrament 'carries the Church's assurance that God is here acting'.[2] This view inverts the logic of the situation: it makes validity the consequence of recognition instead of its condition. In the traditional view that I have expounded, the Church can recognise only those sacraments which it judges to be already valid as a matter of objective fact; in the theory Fr Coventry is describing, the Church's recognition makes them valid. This latter view makes it impossible to explain the traditional distinction between two different unfavourable verdicts which the Church can pass on a sacrament: in addition to the straightforward verdict of invalidity, sacraments have sometimes been considered as of doubtful validity, both of which verdicts imply the Church's refusal of recognition.[3]

A question closely associated with that of validity is that of the Church's power to determine the elements of a sacramental rite which are necessary for the sacrament to be valid. A significant case in point has been the different decisions which have been taken concerning the essentials of the rite of ordination. The Council of Florence in 1439 defined the essential act as the handing over of the instruments of the candidate's office, namely the chalice with the wine and the paten with the bread; in 1947 however Pius XII determined that henceforth the essential rite would be the imposition of the bishop's hands in invocation of the Holy Spirit. Thus an ordination performed without the *traditio instrumentorum* would presumably have been invalid in 1946 and would have needed to be repeated with the prescribed rite; in 1948 however such an ordination would have been valid. However the Church's limited power to vary the *conditions* for the validity of a sacrament does not conflict with the understanding that validity itself is an objective fact independent of the Church's recognition. Whether the Church has the power to change the sacrament of sacerdotal ordination so radically as to apply it to women is of course the fundamental point at issue.

**Watts:** What then does the concept of validity safeguard in the sacramental life of the Church?

**Yarnold:** One thing that the concept of validity guarantees is that God has chosen to convey his grace and his salvation to us not through our own individual efforts but through his Church. If you understand a sacrament as a perceptible and effective symbol of grace which confers what it signifies, the Church itself, as the visible sign of Christ's action in the world, is the fundamental sacrament.[4] The particular sacraments are the moments when the Church's sacramental nature is realised. The insistence on validity expresses this belief that in the sacraments Christ is acting through his Church. This in turn is connected with the visibility of the Church, which not only enables it to be Christ's witness to the world, but to be the palpable means by which Christians share in the life of Jesus Christ, as a body shares in the life of its head. In addition the requirement of a validly ordained minister safeguards the unity of the priesthood and of the Church.

**Watts:** Can one ever have the duty to separate oneself from the communion to which one belongs? What conditions could justify such a step? Is there not a more paramount duty, namely to maintain unity in charity?

**Yarnold:** It seems to me there are two very different possible cases. The first is that of a person who believes that the communion to which one belongs is, for all its human defects, the embodiment of the Church which existed from all eternity in God's saving purpose and in Christ its head–of a person who believes, in the words of Vatican II, that Christ's Church 'subsists in' the church of which he is a member. Such people, I believe, would in no circumstances be justified in voluntarily leaving their church, not so much because of the paramount claims of charity as because they would see themselves to be cutting themselves off from the source of salvation. This attitude would not involve any condemnation of Christians in other communities, but it would imply, to paraphrase the words of St Cyprian, that, for oneself, one would have no right to presume on salvation if one left one's church. If one's conscience disapproves of the actions of the authorities of one's church, one may have the duty to speak against them, and through doing so may even find oneself excommunicated, but one is never justified in *choosing* to depart.

For people who hold this first view, the difference between their church and the others is a difference of kind, as for them one is the 'true Church' and the others are not. Quite different is the position of a person whose choice is not which is the one true Church, but which is the most faithful of several churches, all of which are only incomplete realisations of Christ's will for his Church. Why should not such people remain faithful to the church to which they belong, reluctantly enduring the faults which one cannot correct, as one would do with the faults of a spouse or a son or daughter? Up to a point indeed charity and loyalty imply that this is the right thing to do; otherwise people would be changing churches or spouses every month (though fortunately changing children is not an option). What that point is there is no precise standard for measuring. But one can imagine developments which led one to judge that the church has abandoned Christian principles so radically that one can no longer remain a member of it without being a witness against the truth of the Gospel. Such a position might arise if a church officially abandoned faith in the Incarnation or the Resurrection, or formally allied itself with an unjust political regime.

**Watts:** So would a member of a church be justified in continuing to acknowlege the authority of a bishop who has broken with Catholic order by ordaining women? Would such action compromise his other sacramental ministrations?

**Yarnold:** I shall try to answer the second question first. As far as Roman Catholic canon law is concerned I do not believe that such action would *automatically* invalidate the whole of the bishop's sacramental ministry. I understand that such a situation did arise concerning a Czechoslovakian bishop who, fearing a shortage of priests during communist rule, secretly ordained women. No action could be taken against him, since by the time the matter became public he was no longer alive, but the ordinations were naturally judged invalid. But if the bishop had acted publicly, he would presumably have been suspended or excommunicated, as happened with the Lefebvrist bishops who performed illicit ordinations. Nevertheless if such bishops continued an unauthorised sacramental ministry, the sacraments would be illicit but not invalid. I would judge myself obliged to avoid the ministrations of such bishops even before they were formally suspended or excommunicated. If I were a priest under their obedience I would seek canonical transfer to another diocese; but until then I would judge it right to speak out against their action, while continuing obliged to obey them in all that was not sinful.

It may be helpful to go back to the fifth century and consider St Augustine's attitude to the heretical Donatist bishops. He believed that the baptisms and ordinations of schismatical bishops were valid and unrepeatable, though they could not be means of conferring grace as long as the separation persisted. If they were reconciled with the Catholic Church they did not need to be re-ordained.[5]

**Watts:** A last question. Can a church tolerate the inner division caused by the situation where some of its members regard the orders of some of its ordained ministers to be invalid?

**Yarnold:** The church historian will have no difficulty in finding situations when the church in one part of the world regarded itself as out of communion with the church in another area. What seems to be new in the present circumstances is that it is not a question of one church declaring itself to be out of communion with another because of some deviation on the part of the latter; what we have now is the Church of England with due *legal* form taking an action which as a direct consequence establishes a ministry and therefore a celebration of the Eucharist which one section cannot recognise. An impairment of communion is not *declared* in protest against the action; it is *created* by the action. Whether this is tolerable, Anglicans must judge. The Roman Catholic can only look on, not with *Schadenfreude*, but with empathy and prayer.

**Notes:**

1. This distinction between the *res* and the *res et sacramentum* is a medieval extension of terminology used by St Augustine in the Donatist controversy. For the identification of the *res et sacramentum* as a new or deeper relationship with the Church (the 'ecclesial effect'), see E. Schillebeeckx, *Christ the Sacrament* (London, 1963), pp.190-219.
2. J. Coventry, 'Note on the Mutual Recognition of Ministry', p.80, in *Church Membership and Intercommunion* (ed. J. Kent and R. Murray, London, 1973).
3. Of the papal commission appointed to investigate Anglican Orders in 1896, four members seem to have voted for invalidity, two or three for validity and one or two for 'doubtful validity' (cf. a letter of the future Cardinal Merry del Val, quoted in J. J. Hughes, *Absolutely Null and Utterly Void*, London, 1968, p.162).
4. This was the teaching of the Vatican II Dogmatic Constitution on the Church: 'By her relationship with Christ, the Church is a kind of sacrament or sign of intimate union with God, and of the unity of all mankind' (*Lumen Gentium* 1). The same idea recurs in the ARCIC II document *Church as Communion*: The Church is 'rightly described as a visible sign which both points to and embodies our communion with God and with one another . . . It is a "mystery" or "sacrament"' (n.17).
5. Cf S. L. Greenslade, *Schism in the Early Church* (2nd edn, London, 1964), pp.176-7. Most churches have by now advanced beyond St Augustine's thinking, allowing that the sacramental ministrations of schismatical bishops or priests need not be incapable of conferring grace.

# VII

# Through the Looking Glass: A critique of the legislation relating to the Ordination of Women Priests

## *Lynne Leeder*

"'I know what 'it' means well enough when I find a thing,' said the Duck: 'it's generally a frog or a worm. The question is what did the archbishop find?' '"

Those who listened to the debate in the General Synod which culminated in the approval of the Measure enabling the Church of England to proceed towards the ordination of women priests may be surprised to learn that such ordinations are by no means assured.

Before women can be ordained as priests the Measure has to be approved by both Houses of Parliament and has to receive the Royal Assent. Then the Church has still to obtain the approval of the General Synod for Canons to enable their intention to be carried into effect and for those Canons to be promulged. This also requires the Royal Assent.[2]

During this process considerable attention will be focused upon the Measure that was approved by the General Synod. Such attention was not clearly evident during the debate, as the protagonists concentrated on the substance of the issue rather than its legal form.

It is the intention of this article to indicate a number of difficulties with the current draft legislation, which I believe will cause considerable concern both to the Ecclesiastical Committee of Parliament and to the ecclesiastical and temporal courts when they are asked to interpret the legislation, if it is enacted in its present form. In particular I have sought to highlight a number of areas where the effects of the legislation are unclear, or where the result has been either to reverse the proposed intention or to vary existing parliamentary and ecclesiastical practices. Whilst I have tried to ensure that this analysis is as exhaustive as possible, it is not clear at this stage what further "frogs or worms" may eventually emerge once a full legal examination has been initiated.

## The English Catholic Church

As Peter Newman Brooks has pointed out in his article in this volume, there never has been any real doubt as to the catholicity of the Church of England. It is both a Catholic and a reformed Church. This, together with its established status, gives it a position unique in Christendom, a position which differs even from that of its daughter churches in the USA, Canada and the rest of the world.

England did not experience a Reformation in the same sense as Protestant Europe. The Church of England remains therefore, as it was in origin, two provinces of the Western Catholic Church. In this respect the Church of England is that branch of the true and apostolic Church of Christ which was founded in England when the English were gradually converted to Christianity between the years 597 and 687. [3] Statutes [4] passed during the reign of Henry VIII ousted the jurisdiction of Papal authority and substituted that of Royal Supremacy which gradually itself translated into parliamentary supremacy. Thus great changes occurred in the constitution of the Church of England, which henceforth was recognised as a separate national church. However, there was no intention to depart from the congregation of Christ's Church. [5] The Canon Law of the

Church of England is essentially that of the Roman Catholic Church prior to the Reformation, [6] subject to modifications introduced by statute at the Reformation [7] and subsequently. As such it forms part of the laws of England.[8]

Canon Law is inextricably linked to theology, in which it has its roots. Therefore, in seeking to reach an understanding of any piece of ecclesiastical legislation one must also examine the Church's doctrine. The doctrine of the Church of England is stated to be "grounded in the Holy Scriptures, and in such teachings of the ancient Fathers and Councils of the Church as are agreeable to the said Scriptures. In particular such doctrine is to be found in the Thirty-nine Articles of Religion, the Book of Common Prayer, and the Ordinal".[9]

Provision has been made for the alteration of the outward expression of fundamental doctrine, [10] but the Church of England as the Established Church [11] cannot alter doctrine without the legislative sanction of the state.[12] In common with its laws, the doctrine of the Church of England is tied to the authority of the state and, in the event of conflict,[13] as a matter of law, the will of Parliament, or of the Crown prevails.

## The Legislative Process

Since 1970 the power to initiate legislation by Measure on matters pertaining to the Church of England has been delegated to the General Synod,[14] this power having been conferred initially upon the General Assembly of the Church of England.[15] The General Synod may pass Measures relating to any matter[16] concerning the Church of England,[17] and its powers extend to passing Measures intended to repeal, in whole or in part, any Act of Parliament.[18] In relation to provisions[19] touching doctrinal formulae or the services or ceremonies of the Church of England or the administration of its sacraments or sacred rites, the provisions must be referred to the House of Bishops and submitted for final approval of Synod only in the terms proposed by that House.[20]

Once a proposed Measure has passed through the General

Synod the Legislative Committee of the Synod submits the Measure to the Ecclesiastical Committee of Parliament. [21] The Ecclesiastical Committee must draft a report to Parliament stating the nature and legal effect of the Measure together with the Committee's view upon its expediency. [22] At any time during its consideration of the Measure the Ecclesiastical Committee, either on its own motion, or at the request of the Legislative Committee of the Synod, may invite the Legislative Committee to a conference to discuss the provisions of the Measure. [23] However, the Legislative Committee has no power to vary a Measure, but may withdraw it at any time before presentation to Parliament, either upon its own motion or upon direction from the General Synod. [24] The report of the Ecclesiastical Committee must be communicated in draft to the Legislative Committee and not be presented to Parliament, unless that Committee indicates that it wishes presentation to occur. [25]

Measures of the General Synod are not binding unless they have been laid before Parliament. [26] On a resolution being passed by each House, the Measure, in the form in which it was laid before Parliament, is presented to the Sovereign for the Royal Assent. [27] Once the Royal Assent has been given the Measure has the force and effect of an Act of Parliament. [28]

Those who may be tempted to view the parliamentary procedures relating to Measures as a mere formality would do well to recall that already there are examples this century of Parliament's rejection of Measures which have been presented to it. [29] Critics may argue that in an age when many of the Members of Parliament, if not a majority, are not members of the Church of England, such rejection is inappropriate. However, the fact remains that the Ecclesiastical Committee must report its view to Parliament of the expediency of Measures presented to it. Further, in the absence of any powers vested either in the Ecclesiastical Committee or Parliament to amend a measure, it must stand or fall in the form presented by the General Synod.

## By What Authority?

Given the above, does the national church have a duty to look beyond its own boundaries when considering legislation? In one sense the answer is clearly no, because, as we have seen, so far as the law of England is concerned, the Church of England may, with the sanction of the State, do as it pleases. Yet the Church of England remains a catholic Church and, being so, cannot but look past narrow territorial boundaries to the wider Church beyond.

Early Christian writers applied the term "Catholic" to the universal Church. However, gradually it acquired the technical meaning of the "Great Church", which was the guardian of tradition against the many heretical sects which had broken away. This is still the view held by many Anglicans who believe that no single communion can claim such an exclusive title as its own. The term "Catholic" is to be applied therefore to all those churches which maintain the faith and traditions of the Creeds, the Ecumenical Councils and the Church Fathers, together with the practice of the Sacraments and the Episcopate in historical succession from the Apostles.

This matter was considered in the report of the Commission on Christian Doctrine appointed by the Archbishops of Canterbury and York in 1922. They stated that:

> "the inclusive unity for which the term "Catholic" stands implies that the Church is supra-national.... the appeal to the Catholic Church or to catholic tradition appears to us to involve in modern circumstances a refusal to become wholly immersed in the tradition of any one Christian communion, and a determination to recognise the experience and teaching of Christendom as a whole as possessing more fully than any partial system the authority of the Catholic Church. It is the mark of a sectarian mind to refuse to acknowledge what is of permanent truth and value in the tradition of other communions; the "Catholic" should never be "sectarian" however large the

"sect" to which he belongs. The term "Catholic" also implies the conviction that according to Divine Will the true Church on earth was from the beginning and was meant to continue doctrinally and sacramentally, as well as spiritually, one."[30]

Whilst the reports of such commissions are not binding, they have always been held to be authoritative.

Many within the Church of England fear that the decision to ordain women as priests will rob the Church of England of its claim to be part of the Catholic Church, having thereby departed from its faith and tradition. Conscious of past schism the Church of England strove from its foundation to impose upon its members a duty to avoid occasions of strife, a stipulation carried into the current, revised Canons of the Church.[31] Yet clearly that is what will occur if women are ordained as priests.

Not only will such a step lead inevitably to a "serious erosion"[32] of the degree of communion already existing between the Church of England and the Roman Catholic, Orthodox and Ancient Oriental Churches, but, in addition, many Anglican clergy will be forced to resign as a result of their adherence to a doctrine held by the Church since its inception. Indeed the likelihood of such schism is recognised in the legislation itself.[33]

It has been argued by some that, had the Church of England refused to ordain women, in the long term it would have found itself suffering impaired communion with its daughter churches within the wider Anglican communion. However, at the present time it is unlikely that all the Anglican churches will ordain women and therefore the Church of England would not be alone in that communion if it elected not to do so.

Nor can it be argued that the Church of England would have been promoting schism within its own ranks had the General Synod rejected the Measure. Any decision to leave the Church on the part of the supporters of women's ordination would have been the result of disagreement with the doctrine held by the Church when they themselves elected to become communicant members. Schism is the result of action not inaction. It results from change rather than from adherence to tradition.

It has been a matter of dispute whether or not the question of the ordination of women is a matter of doctrine. Taking doctrine to mean that which is taught or a body of instruction, including beliefs, dogma and tenets of the Church, then the answer must surely be in the affirmative. As we have seen already alteration of the doctrine of the Church of England can be made only with the sanction of the State. Curiously perhaps, the national Church can alter doctrine, whereas other churches which do not enjoy the status of establishment cannot. Many of these churches–comprised of a voluntary association of christians– have by the manner in which they came into being fettered themselves to such an extent that they may not seek to alter their doctrines.[34]

However, a question must be raised about the extent to which a church, in seeking to amend its doctrine, risks losing its identity. In this respect it may be instructive to consider briefly the case of the *Free Church of Scotland v Overtoun*.[35] There a dispute arose between the members of the Free Church of Scotland, resulting in legal action which reached the House of Lords. A small minority of members alleged that a breach of trust had occurred in relation to the assets of that church. The dispute arose out of the wish of the majority to unite themselves with the United Presbyterian Church to form a single body to be known as the United Free Church to whom the trustees of the Free Church of Scotland proposed to transfer its property. This unification involved a change of doctrine within the Free Church which the minority who brought the action asserted the church was not entitled to do. This view was upheld by the majority of their Lordships. Although different principles applied in respect of a voluntary association as opposed to an established church, [36] passages from the speeches of their Lordships may shed some light upon the current dilemma. In particular there are the often-cited remarks of the Earl of Halsbury:

"Speaking generally, one would say that the identity

of a religious community described as a Church must consist in the unity of its doctrines. Its creeds, confessions, formularies, tests and so forth are apparently intended to ensure the unity of the faith which its adherents profess."[37]

Lord James recognised the problem when he said:

"I think it worthy of remark that the Church is not a positive, defined entity as would be the case if it were a corporation created by law. It is a body of men united by the possession of common opinion and if this community of opinion ceases to exist, the foundations of the Church give way".[38]

While the first part of his observation may not be applicable to the Church of England one cannot but wonder at the appositeness of the later part. The difficulty is taken up again by the Earl of Halsbury:

"Assuming as I do that there are differences of belief between them,[39] these differences are not got rid of by their agreeing to say nothing about them, nor are these essentially diverse views avoided by selecting so elastic a formulary as can be accepted by people who differ and say that they claim their liberty to retain their differences whilst purporting to join in one Christian Church . . . . Such an agreement would not, in my view, constitute a Church at all, or it would be, to use Sir William Smith's phrase, a Church without a religion."[40]

We have traced the legislative process of the Church of England and examined how this inter-relates with the fundamental presuppositions of the Church. It is clear from an examination of the powers given to the General Synod that it was never the intention of Parliament to delegate an unfettered and unsupervised power to legislate. However, it must be a matter of some surprise to discover that the doctrines of the Established Church may prove to rest on shifting sands by comparison with the rocks which are the foundations of many of the non-established churches. In this respect can it be said that already the Church of England has passed through the looking glass?

## The Proposed Legislation

The Proposed Legislation relating to the ordination of women to the Priesthood is contained in two draft Measures, the Priests (Ordination of Women) Measure and the Ordination of Women (Financial Provisions) Measure. The comments which follow are divided into general areas of discussion, rather than by reference to the section numbers contained within the draft legislation.

### *Financial Provision*

The Measure making financial provision was passed in order to seek to comply with the requirements of section 12 of the main Measure, which states that provision be made for the relief from hardship of those resigning from ecclesiastical service by reason of their opposition to the ordination of women priests. Whether it will, in fact, achieve its stated objective has been doubted by many, who see its provisions as making inadequate financial provision for those who resign. It should be noted however that there is no intention to transfer any of the substantive property of the Church to those who may resign. Whilst this may be acceptable as far as individuals are concerned, it calls into question the treatment of parishes where all or a majority are opposed to the ordination of women and, as a result, propose to leave the Church of England. Such parishes will lose their place of worship together with the residence in which their priest lives. Thus the fabric of the life of the parish, to which, no doubt, the parishioners will themselves have contributed, financially and in other ways, will be removed, together with the financial support previously available from central funds and other bodies. The proposal, put forward by some of those opposed to the ordination of women, for the creation of a third province, alongside Canterbury and York, which did not permit the ordination of women and accordingly to whose authority such parishes could submit, has so far been rejected. Those who decline to consider such a proposal have not put forward any alternative which would provide for an equitable division of the assets of the Church.

The law relating to property, and in particular ecclesiastical property is complex and beyond the scope of an article such as this. Briefly however, it may be said that the manner in which ecclesiastical property is held falls under three broad heads. First, property may be vested in persons in a representative capacity for spiritual or other purposes in connection with a parish.[41] Secondly property may be held by a corporation[42] or some other legally constituted body as trustee for the benefit of the Church of England as a whole.[43] Thirdly, it may be held on the same basis for specified purposes, persons, or territories (other than parishes) within the Church. Depending upon its exact nature and the terms upon which it is held, some of the property held under the first two heads may become the subject of legal action. Currently attention is focused on the third head where disputes as to the disposition of certain funds have arisen already.[44]

## Bishops

The draft Measure allows for the possibility of "a bishop of a diocese in office at the relevant date" making any one or more of three declarations. First, that a woman is not to be ordained to the office of priest within the diocese; secondly, that a woman is not to be instituted or licensed to the office of incumbent or priest-in-charge of a benefice, or team vicar for a benefice within the diocese; finally, that a woman is not to be given a licence or permission to officiate as a priest within the diocese.[45]

At first reading, the expression "a bishop", as opposed to "the bishop", of a diocese, may well be interpreted to include suffragan bishops, yet the scheme of the section supports the view that it is intended only to apply to diocesan bishops.[46] What then is the position of a suffragan bishop whose views on this issue do not coincide with those of his diocesan bishop? Clearly he cannot act in contravention of any such declaration made by his diocesan,[47] not least because it is contemplated that to do so would constitute an offence in ecclesiastical law.[48] Yet what of the reverse situation, where a suffragan is opposed to the ordination of women priests and his diocesan issues none of the contemplated declarations? It is not a question to which it appears possible to give an adequate answer at this juncture. Much may depend upon the terms of the diocesan's commission to his suffragan,[49] but ultimately it may well transpire that the position of any such suffragan is untenable and that he will feel obliged to resign from office.

A further difficulty in the proposed legislation in this area is the phrase "in office at the relevant date".[50] The relevant date is clearly defined[51] but what is intended by the requirement to be "in office"? Does it mean that a bishop must occupy the office of bishop of the diocese for which he makes the declaration[52] or so long as he was in office as *a* bishop of *a* diocese at the relevant date, may issue declarations in any diocese to which he is later translated? This second interpretation may go some way to explain the choice of *a* as opposed to "*the* bishop of a diocese" in the opening words of the section discussed above, and might thus extend to suffragans, in office at the relevant date, and later appointed as diocesan bishops. Each option presents difficulties. If the latter is correct then the possibility of a bishop opposed to the ordination of women priests accepting office in a new diocese, as diocesan bishop, is severely restricted, since presumably he could take office only in a diocese in which his predecessor had issued declarations identical with those he would propose to issue himself, if he did not wish to find himself in an invidious position.

If the former interpretation is correct then effectively such bishops will not be able to take any new office. In practice such distinctions, if they become relevant, will operate for only a short time. The thrust of the proposed legislation is quite clear; that in time no bishop will raise impediments either to the ordination of women to the priesthood or to the exercise of their ministry within his diocese.

This of course presents grave difficulties for those opposed to the ordination of women and in particular raises concerns about their representation in the governing bodies of the Church. If the draft Measure does become law, then, in less than twenty years, it is unlikely that any bishop will be legally capable of issuing such declarations. The intention behind such provisions is obviously that, in time, all bishops will ordain, institute and licence women priests within their diocese. Precisely how the Church will compel a bishop to do so is far from clear, other than by the judicious selection of candidates when a vacancy arises. [53]

A possible solution to the issue of the representation of those opposed to the ordination of women to the priesthood in the House of Bishops of the General Synod and in the Upper Houses of the two Convocations may be provided, in due course, under the terms of alternative episcopal oversight. As a matter of practice however it is likely that a two-tier church will be created with those opposed to the ordination of women not being given a effective voice within the Church. Undoubtedly this will change the nature of the Church and in time will affect its liturgy and theology.

## *Parishes*

The scheme of the legislation permits parochial church councils[54] to pass either or both of two resolutions; [55] namely that they would not accept a woman as the incumbent or priest-in-charge of the benefice or as a team vicar for the benefice or that they would not accept a woman as the minister who presides at or celebrates Holy Communion or pronounces the Absolution in the parish. Unlike the proposals relating to bishops there are no restrictions equivalent to the requirement to be in office at the relevant date. Presumably it is envisaged that some parishes may remain permanently opposed to the ministry of women priests. It would appear to be open to a parish not merely to rescind such resolutions[56] but also to opt for them at some point in the future, even in certain circumstances where the current incumbent, priest-in-charge or team vicar was a woman.[57] This must be a matter of some concern as it could lead to a situation of total stalemate in a parish, the outcome of which is unclear.

Although curtailments already exist affecting the rights of patrons to present the candidate of their choice to a benefice, the proposed legislation carries with it further restrictions, although their full impact is far from apparent. Most obviously a patron could not seek to present a woman to a benefice in contravention of either a resolution passed by the parochial church council or a declaration issued by the relevant bishop.[58]

What however of those parishes where the patron is opposed to the ordination of women to the priesthood, but in which the parochial church council make clear that their tradition is such[59] that they would welcome an incumbent who was a woman or was in favour of women priests? Would the parochial representatives or the bishop be within their rights to refuse their approval to a candidate whose opposition to the ordination of women to the priesthood was the only ground for their refusal? Likewise would the Archbishop be entitled to uphold a refusal made by a bishop on this basis, if he is ultimately requested by the patron to review such a decision.[60] Further, what would be the attitude of the courts should a patron seek a remedy for the disturbance of his rights?[61] In practice no parochial church council or bishop would be advised to state their grounds of refusal in such a way as to leave them open to review.

Another difficulty arising from the proposed legislation will be the creation and operation of pastoral schemes. Amendments to the Pastoral Measure 1983[62] seek to meet some of the potential difficulties but questions remain unresolved. Presumably those parochial church councils which pass resolutions in both of the forms available to them have objections to women priests above and beyond their presiding at or celebrating Holy Communion or pronouncing the Absolution. Yet, if their parish is, or becomes part of a group ministry, while presumably they will be protected from their own incumbent being a woman[63] and from any other incumbent within the group, who is a woman, presiding at or celebrating Holy Communion or pronouncing Absolution[64] all incumbents within the group, whether male or female, and regardless of their views upon the issue, have authority to perform all such other offices and services in that parish.[65] Thus, for example, a woman incumbent from the group could conduct marriages or take evensong.

In respect of team ministries it is proposed that no woman who is a vicar in a team shall have authority to preside at or celebrate Holy Communion or to pronounce the Absolution, where the parochial church council has issued a resolution against such occurring.[66] There is no specific provision however to take account of the situation in which a parish forming part of a team ministry, has passed a resolution to the effect that it would not accept a woman as incumbent, or as a team vicar. Thus in parishes which form part of a team it would appear that a woman could become an incumbent or one of the team vicars against the will of the parish.

The practical solution must lie in the fact that the main legislation envisages that no person may act in contravention of resolutions passed by a parochial church council[67] and indeed, for the clergy to do so would constitute an ecclesiastical offence.[68] However the confusion arising is likely to make the creation of any new pastoral schemes a minefield in both legal and pastoral terms. Problems may develop also in respect of the continuance of existing schemes. Parishes of differing traditions simply may not be able to co-exist within one scheme and the danger of merging parishes in which the tradition of one may be overlaid by that of the other is all too obvious.

It can be assumed also that a parochial church council which issued such resolutions would require a priest who was himself opposed to the ordination of women in accordance with the "traditions" of the parish.[69] Yet it is difficult to see how either such a minister, or the parish as a whole, could submit to the episcopal authority of a bishop who did not share their beliefs on this issue. For the minister, in particular, this could have potentially grave implications, since disobedience to the lawful commands of the bishop could constitute an ecclesiastical offence.[70] A solution has been mooted, although not in the current draft legislation, of alternative episcopal oversight. The possible form this might take and the manifold legal and pastoral complications arising from such proposals, form the subject matter of an article in themselves[71] and it is not proposed to consider them here.

## Interpretation

The draft Measure contains one general statement of interpretation,[72] together with a number of minor and consequential amendments,[73] relating to the ordination of women priests. Despite these it would appear that a number of anomalies exist. It is intended that in any Canon, order, rule or regulation relating to priests, words importing the masculine gender include the feminine, unless the contrary intention appears.[74] No mention is made however of either Acts of Parliament or of Measures of the Church Assembly or the General Synod, which are, in fact, interpreted so far as its provisions extend to them by the Interpretation Act 1978[75]. This leads to a confused situation which is complicated still further by the failure of the proposed draft Measure to provide that so far as Canons, orders, rules or regulations are concerned, words importing the feminine gender include the masculine.[76] So far as certain sections of various Measures are concerned some of the resulting difficulties are removed by the inclusion of specific amendments.[77]

Unless a thorough examination of the entire legislation relating to the Church of England is undertaken a number of anomalies will remain.[78] In particular the seeming failure by the Church to explore fully the implications of English and European Community Law in the field of sex discrimination and equal treatment is rendered all the more curious in the light of arguments by some of the supporters of the legislation who sought to equalise treatment as between men and women in the Church.[79]

Perhaps the most potentially dangerous aspect of the legislation is the reliance upon the repeal, by implication, of part of section 10 of the Act of Uniformity. This provides that no person shall be capable of being admitted to any "parsonage vicarage benefice or other ecclesiastical promotion or dignity before such time as *he* shall be ordained priest...." Certainly since the Act was prior to 1850, the provisions of the Interpretation Act 1978 do not enable one simply to read words importing the masculine gender as including the feminine.[80] It is interesting to note that similar problems arose, so far as the appointment of deacons to certain positions was concerned, following the enactment of the Deacons (Ordination of Women) Measure 1986. There specific legislation had to be enacted eventually to resolve the consequent confusion.[81]

With modern legislation it is not the practice to rely upon repeal by implication. Where it is appreciated that this must be the actual effect of a proposed provision or provisions, a specific clause expressly repealing the relevant statement is generally included. In this case the Church cannot claim that it was unaware of the implications of this Measure and therefore it seems clear that it is content to rely upon the implicit repeal of one of its earliest and most fundamental statutes. Whilst the Church may be so content, the Ecclesiastical Committee or indeed Parliament as a whole, may well feel otherwise.

## Conclusion

Such is the manifest ambiguity of the proposed legislation that it cannot be satisfactory that it should pass into law in its present form. Whatever one's opinion about the question of the ordination of women, it can profit no section of the Church to set out upon such a difficult journey when it is known that the road is built upon sand. Surely it would be preferable for the Legislative Committee, either on its own motion or on the direction of the General Synod, to withdraw the draft Measures and for Synod to seek to resolve the many difficulties. If the Measures were to be considered again surely it would be helpful if at the same time as the substantive proposals were reviewed, concrete provisions were introduced to facilitate the practical implementation of the ordination of women. Otherwise, like Lewis Carroll's Dodo, one is left saying, "the best way to explain it is to do it."[82]

## Notes

1. Lewis Carroll "*Alice in Wonderland*", chapter 3.
2. Submission of the Clergy Act 1533, s.1; Synodical Government Measure 1969, s.1(3)(a), Sch.2, art 6(a)(ii).
3. *Halsbury's Laws of England*, 4th edn, vol 14; Ecclesiastical Law, para 345; Marshall v Graham [1907] 2KB 112 at 126, DC.
4. Ecclesiastical Appeals Act 1532 (repealed); Submission of the Clergy Act 1533 (part repealed); Appointments of Bishops Act 1533 (part repealed); Ecclesiastical Licences Act 1533 (part repealed); 26 Hen. 8c. 1 (Supremacy of the Crown) (1534) (repealed).
5. *Halsbury's Laws of England*, 4th edn, vol 14; Ecclesiastical Law, para 345, n.2; Marshall v Graham [1907] 2KB 112 at 126, DC.
6. In the English Ecclesiastical Courts all earlier canons, save those relating to purely local matters, were superseded by the codification of the canon law in the *Corpus Juris Canonici*, which was the foundation of the *jus commune*. After the *Decretum Gratiani*, c.1150, (the beginning of the *Corpus Juris Canonici*) such canons as were made in England were solely for the purpose of emphasising rules of the *Corpus Juris Canonici* and of applying them to local needs and enforcing them: *Halsbury's Laws of England*, 4th edn, vol 14; Ecclesiastical Law, para 305. The canon law of Papal Rome, as applied within the Realm of England, subject to local modifications, never formed, as a body of laws, part of the law of England; This was the unanimous opinion of the judges advising the House of Lords in R v Millis (1844) 10 Cl & Fin 534, where the House itself was equally divided. The judges' opinion was however quoted by Blackburn J in his advice to the House of Lords in Bishop of Exeter v Marshall (1868) LR 3 HL 17, and expressly approved by Lord Chelmsford LC, at 46.
7. At the Reformation such of the canon law as applied in England and was not "repugnant, contrariant or derogatory" to the laws or statutes of the realm, nor to the prerogatives of the Crown, received statutory recognition: 35 Hen. 8 c. 16 (Canon Law) (1543) (repealed); Submission of the Clergy Act 1533, s.7 (repealed); Read v Bishop of Lincoln (1889) Roscoe's Rep 1 at 17.
8. Its authority depends not upon statutory recognition but upon its incorporation as such into the laws of the land at the Reformation; *Halsbury's Laws of England*, 4th edn, vol 14; Ecclesiastical Law, para 306.
9. *The Canons of the Church of England*, Canons Ecclesiastical promulged by the Convocations of Canterbury and York in 1964 and 1969 and by the General Synod of the Church of England from 1970 (Church House Publishing, 4th edn 1986 incorporating supplements 1/4, April 1987/April 1990), henceforward referred to as "Canons of the Church of England"; Ibid Canon A5.
10. Both the Preface to the *Book of Common Prayer* and Article of Religion 34 recognise that forms of divine worship and the rites and ceremonies appointed to be used in the public liturgy of the Church of England may be altered in certain circumstances. The Church of England (Worship and Doctrine) Measure 1974, s. 1(1), provides for the power of the General Synod to approve, amend, continue or discontinue forms of service, by canon.
11. *Canons of the Church of England*, Canon A1.

12. It is this freedom from control which differentiates a voluntary association from an established church: General Assembly of the Free Church of Scotland v Lord Overtoun [1904] AC 515 at 648, HL.

13. As, eg. Parliament's rejection of the Revised Prayer Books, put forward, in proposed Measures, by the Church Assembly in 1927 & 1928.

14. Synodical Government Measure 1969, s.2(1), sch.2, art.6(a)(i).

15. Church of England Assembly (Powers) Act 1919.

16. It has been assumed generally that Parliament, in granting to the Church Assembly the power to pass Measures relating to "matters concerning the Church of England", gave the Assembly powers in the widest terms. Whether such was in fact the intention of Parliament must be a matter of some doubt. The bill which subsequently became the Church of England Assembly (Powers) Act 1919, was promoted to relieve a situation which had become such that the Church had been unable, for some years, to put forward legislation because Parliament did not have the time to devote to it. It was said that the bill would assist the Church to deal with the log jam of legislation without which the administration of the Church would be greatly hampered. From the debates in both Houses of Parliament it is clear that concern was expressed over the use of the term "matter" in preference to a more specific definition of the subject matters which Parliament foresaw as being appropriate to the new procedure. Alternative terms were rejected on the basis that Parliament might otherwise fetter the Assembly on issues which were intended to be within its competence, eg. certain property matters. It was said by the Archbishop of Canterbury that the bill was to deal with the outer secular rules of the Church not spiritual fundamentals such as the doctrines of the faith. If, in fact, some greater limitations than are presently thought to exist, were intended in relation to the subject matter of Measures then Parliament has held the power to initiate fundamental legislative changes solely to itself. In view of Parliamentary Supremacy, whether by means of Act of Parliament or in relation to Measures, the point may well appear academic. However, it may also be indicative of the fact that the Church's powers may not be as great as the majority suppose.

17. Church of England (Assembly) Powers Act 1919, s.3(6); Synodical Government Measure 1969, s.2(2), Sch.2 art.6(a)(i). General Synod may also make provision by canon, made in exercise of the powers transferred from the Convocations of Canterbury and York to General Synod, by such order, regulation or other subordinate instrument as may be authorised by Measure or canon, by Act of Synod, regulation, or other instrument or proceedings as may be appropriate in cases where provision by or under a Measure or canon is not required: Ibid., Sch.2, art.6(a).

18. Including the Church of England Assembly (Powers) Act 1919, but a Measure must not provide for any alteration in the composition or powers or duties of the Ecclesiastical Committee of Parliament or the procedure prescribed by Parliament for its own consideration of Measures reported on by the Ecclesiastical Committee: Church of England Assembly (Powers) Act 1919, s.3(6); Synodical Government Measure 1969, s.2(2).

19. "Provision" includes canons and Acts of Synod as well as Measures: Ibid., s.2(1), Sch.2, art.12(1).

20. Ibid., Sch.2, art.7(1). If either of the Convocations of Canterbury or York or the House of Laity so require, a provision relating to these matters must be referred, in the terms proposed by the House of Bishops for final approval, to the two Convocations sitting separately for their provinces and to the House of Laity who must, if the provision is to be submitted for final approval by General Synod, approve it in the terms proposed by the House of Bishops: Ibid., Sch.2 art.7 (2), (3), (4). In the absence of approval by each of the four Houses of Convocation or by the House of Laity, standing orders of the General Synod must provide that such a provision is not put forward again in the same, or in a similar form, until a new General Synod comes into being: Ibid., Sch 2., art.7 (5), save that in the event that approval is not given by one House of one Convocation provision exists for a second reference to the Convocations and in the case of a second refusal by one House, for reference to the Houses of Bishops and Clergy of General Synod for approval by a two-thirds majority of the members of each House present and voting, in lieu of approval by the four Houses: Sch 2., art.7(5). In addition no canon making provision with respect to worship or doctrine may be submitted for the assent and licence of the Sovereign unless it has been finally approved by General Synod with a majority in each House of not less than two thirds of those present and voting, and no regulation under any canon with respect to worship, nor any approval, amendment, continuance or discontinuance of a form of service by General Synod under any such canon is to have effect unless the regulation, the form of service or the amendment, continuance or discontinuance has been finally approved by General Synod with a majority in each House of not less than two thirds of those present and voting: Church of England (Worship and Doctrine) Measure 1974 ss. 1(1), 2(1) & 3.

21. Measures which the General Synod wishes to pass into law are referred to its Legislative Committee which must submit the Measure to the Ecclesiastical Committee of Parliament, together with such comments and explanations as the Legislative Committee either deem expedient, or are directed by General Synod, to add: Church of England Assembly (Powers) Act 1919, s.3(1); Synodical Government Measure 1969, s.2(2).

22. Especially in relation to the constitutional rights of all Her Majesty's subjects: Church of England Assembly (Powers) Act 1919, s.3(3).

23. Ibid., s.3(2). After which a conference of the two committees must take place.

24. Ibid., s.3(4).

25. Ibid., s.3(5); Synodical Government Measure 1969, s.2(2).

26. Once the report of the Ecclesiastical Committee has been made to Parliament the report, together with the text of the Measure, is laid before both Houses forthwith if Parliament is sitting, or if not, then after the next meeting of Parliament: Church of England Assembly (Powers) Act 1919, s.4.

27. Parliament has no power to amend a Measure, only to pass or decline to pass a resolution that the Measure be presented to the Sovereign.

28. Church of England Assembly (Powers) Act 1919, s.4.

29. cf. n.13.

30. "*Doctrine in the Church of England*", The Report of the Commission on Christian Doctrine appointed by the Archbishops of Canterbury and York in 1922, SPCK, 1938, p.110.

31. *Canons of the Church of England,* Canon A8.
32. The expression is taken from a letter written by His Holiness John Paul II to the Most Reverend Robert Runcie, Archbishop of Canterbury on 8 December 1988.
33. Draft Ordination of Women (Financial Provisions) Measure.
34. General Assembly of the Free Church of Scotland and Others v Lord Overtoun and Others [1904] AC 515, HL. per Earl Halsbury LC.
35. Ibid.
36. Although there was much discussion about the adherence of the Free Church to the establishment principle it was not an established church. The question at issue was the ascertainment of the principles upon which the Free Church had been founded and, in particular, what powers it had given itself, if any, upon inception to alter those principles.
37. General Assembly of the Free Church of Scotland and Others v Lord Overtoun and Others [1904] AC 515, at 612.
38. Ibid., at 656.
39. "them" being the Free Church of Scotland and The United Presbyterian Church.
40. General Assembly of the Free Church of Scotland and Others v Lord Overtoun and Others [1904] AC 515, at 627.
41. In order to ensure that property is permanently devoted to a particular purpose ecclesiastical it is generally vested in an ecclesiastical corporation which is recognised by law as having a permanent capacity by reason of an office or of the function of holding property. Such corporations are either a corporation sole or a corporation aggregate: 1 Bl Com (14th edn) 70. Examples of corporations sole are bishops and incumbents, (including rectors, vicars and perpetual curates and rectors and vicars of new benefices created by pastoral schemes) and parochial church councils: Parochial Church Councils (Powers) Measure 1956, s.3.
42. The trustees of any charity for religious purposes may apply to the Charity Commissioners to be registered as a body corporate: Charitable Trustees Incorporation Act 1872, s.1.
43. E.g. the Church Commissioners to whom the funds of the Corporation of Queen Anne's Bounty and the common fund of the Ecclesiastical Commissioners were transferred.
44. Detailed examples of these cannot be given as it is anticipated that legal proceedings may be commenced.
45. Draft Priests (Ordination of Women) Measure, s.2(1).
46. The declarations set out in Ibid., s.2(1) apply to the diocese as a whole, and there is no provision by which such declarations must be notified to the diocesan bishop, as would surely be the case if a suffragan could make such declarations: Ibid., s.2(4).
47. Ibid., s.2(6).
48. Ibid., s.5(a).
49. Suffragan Bishops Act 1534, s.4; *Canons of the Church of England,* Canon C20.
50. Draft Priests (Ordination of Women) Measure, s.2(1).
51. Ibid., s.2(8).
52. Arguably so if one reads back "the diocese" from each of the three declarations set out in the text of the sub-section.

53. All diocesan bishops in England are appointed by the Crown, either by royal letters missive and *conge d'élire,* or exceptionally, if the dean and chapter or cathedral chapter defer the election (or in the diocese of Sodor and Man where there is no chapter) by letters patent: Appointment of Bishops Act 1533, ss.3, 4; Cathedrals Measure 1931, ss.3, 23(3). The Appointment of Bishops Act 1533 does not on the face of it contemplate that the archbishop may, in any way, question the fitness of the person nominated by the Crown, and in "confirming" the candidate would appear to act purely as a ministerial agent: R v Archbishop of Canterbury [1902] 2 KB 503. Objections may be taken on two grounds only, namely that the election has been defective in form and that the person presented for confirmation is not the person whom the Crown has chosen; Ibid. The only means by which anyone may raise an objection is to petition the Crown not to issue its mandate for confirmation: Dr Temple's Case (1869) Times 9 December 1869.

54. And in the case of parishes in which there is a parish church cathedral and in respect of which the functions of the parochial church council were transferred to the administrative body of the cathedral, in pursuance of the Cathedrals Measure 1963, s.12, that administrative body.

55. Draft Priests (Ordination of Women) Measure, s.3(1), sch.1.

56. Ibid., s.3(2).

57. Ibid, s.3(3) states that a resolution to the effect that the parochial church council would not accept a woman as the minister who presides at or celebrates Holy Communion or pronounces the Absolution in the parish, shall not be considered if the incumbent or priest-in-charge of the benefice concerned or any team vicar or assistant curate for that benefice is a woman priest. Surprisingly the parochial church council is not estopped from considering the alternative resolution, namely that they would not accept a woman as the incumbent or priest-in-charge of the benefice or team vicar for the benefice, in identical circumstances. No doubt it was envisaged by those who framed the draft legislation that such a declaration would be issued only in a situation where a vacancy had, or was about to arise. What however would be the position if such a resolution were passed when no vacancy was anticipated and the then incumbent priest-in-charge or a team vicar was a woman. Does "accept" connote a once and for all time action and thus the woman minister, having been accepted initially, cannot later be rejected? Certainly the legal implications of any attempt to remove a woman minister, if such a resolution were passed, are far-reaching. An incumbent has security of tenure having, by induction, been put into complete possession of the church and benefice with all the profits and emoluments. Similarly a team vicar enjoys the same security of tenure as an incumbent: Pastoral Measure 1983, s.20 (3). Whilst an incumbent may be deprived of a benefice when he is disqualified by law from holding it, such deprivation normally arises either as the result of the appointment being tainted by simony (with or without the incumbent's knowledge), or the commission by the incumbent of some offence, or as a result of some incapacity, of either mind or body, of the incumbent. Whether the issue by a parochial parish council of a declaration would be sufficient to disqualify in law a minister already appointed is a moot point and one which ultimately may have to be answered by the Courts, if the legislation is enacted. The situation is

complicated further by the proposal that it should be an ecclesiastical offence for any bishop, priest or deacon to act, or to permit any act, in contravention of either of the resolutions which may be passed by a parochial church council, to be committed in any church or building licensed for public worship according to the rites and ceremonies of the Church of England; Draft Priests (Ordination of Women) Measure, s.5(b). There is also the fact that Ibid., s.3(6) states that where such resolutions are in force a person discharging any function in relation to the parish or benefice concerned shall not act in contravention of the resolutions. It is doubtful whether these provisions could amount to a disqualification in law, but it would place any woman minister in a position whereby she could not exercise her ministry. Further no other minister may exercise their ministry in any place in which they do not have the cure of souls without the permission of the minister having such cure, and the minister who has the cure of souls may not allow another minister to minister within their church or chapel for a period of more than seven days within three months without reference to the bishop or other Ordinary: *Canons of the Church of England*, Canon C8, paras 2(a), (4). That such an anomaly could have arisen at all is curious if one compares the provisions relating to the declarations which it is proposed may be issued by the administrative body of a cathedral church. Despite the fact that the resolutions are in broadly similar terms to those discussed above, a motion for either resolution may not be considered if a dean or any of the residentiary canons of the cathedral church is a woman ordained to the office of priest: draft Priests (Ordination of Women) Measure, s.4(3).

58. Ibid., ss. 2(1), 3(1), (6).
59. Patronage (Benefices) Measure 1986, s.11(1)(a).
60. Ibid., s.13(4), (5).
61. The remedies a patron may seek for disturbance of the right of patronage are by:-
    (a) appeal to the Court, where the refusal to institute or admit is on the grounds of unfitness or disqualification sufficient in law to justify a refusal, except a ground of doctrine or ritual: Benefices Act 1898, s.3; Patronage (Benefices) Measure 1986, s.18(1)(a); (b) an action in the nature of a *quare impedit*, brought in the temporal courts, where the refusal is on the grounds of doctrine or ritual, or certain other grounds: Benefices Act 1898, s.3; Heywood v Bishop of Manchester (1884) 12 QBD 404; Gore-Booth v Bishop of Manchester [1920] 2 KB 412; affd. 89 LJKB 1128, CA; Statute Law (Repeals) Act 1969, s.2; (c) a suit of *duplex querela*, in the Court of Ecclesiastical Causes Reserved, again if refusal is on the grounds of doctrine or ritual, or if on some other ground of law the bishop fails to signify his refusal in writing or if the refusal is on a ground insufficient in law to justify the refusal: Benefices Act 1898, s.3 (1), (5); Benefices Act 1972, s. 2; Ecclesiastical Jurisdiction Measure 1963, s.10 (1)(b). Of course it could be that a Court will have to ascertain, as a preliminary point, whether or not the refusal was in fact based upon a ground of doctrine.
62. Draft Priests (Ordination of women) Measure, s.10, sch. 3, paras 6, 7.
63. By virtue of their resolution B: Ibid., s.3(1), sch 1.
64. By the proposed amendments to the Pastoral Measure 1983, s. 21(1).
65. Ibid., s.21(1)(a), as amended by the draft Priests (Ordination of Women) Measure, s.10, sch.3, para. 7.

66. Ibid., s.10, sch.3, para 6, by amending the Pastoral Measure 1983, s.20(8).
67. Draft Priests (Ordination of Women) Measure, s.3(6).
68. Ibid., s.5(b).
69. Patronage (Benefices) Measure 1986, s.11(1)(a).
70. Godolphin's *Reportorium Canonicum* 307; Rugg v Bishop of Winchester (1868) LR 2 PC 223.
71. cf. "Alternative Episcopal Oversight" by John Rees.
72. Draft Priests (Ordination of Women) Measure, s.9.
73. Ibid., s.10, sch.3.
74. Ibid., s.9.
75. The Interpretation Act 1978 applies to all Measures of the General Synod and Acts of Parliament passed after 1st January 1979: Ibid., s.22, sch.2, part I. As regards earlier legislation (including Measures of the Church Assembly passed after 28th May 1925) only certain provisions of the Interpretation Act apply: Ibid, s.22(1), sch. 2, part I. Thus in all Acts and Measures passed after the year 1850 "words importing the masculine gender include the feminine": Ibid., s.6(a), sch.2, part I, and in Acts and Measures passed after 1st January 1979 "words importing the feminine gender include the masculine": Ibid., s.6(2), sch 2, part I.
76. Thus eg. "wife" cannot be read as husband, although the converse may apply.
77. cf. n.73.
78. Eg. The Pluralities Act 1838, ss.29 & so, (relating to prohibitions against those in Holy Orders engaging in certain trading activities) remains unamended even though ss. 36 & 43 are intended to be specifically amended: draft Priests (Ordination of Women) Measure, s.10, sch.3, paras. 1, 2. Also a man may be deprived from holding any preferment following certain secular proceedings such as divorce or judicial separation where his wife is entitled to rely upon various matters: Ecclesiastical Jurisdiction Measure 1963, s.55(1)(b).
79. cf. n.78. The anomalies referred to above lead in fact to more favourable treatment for women in Holy Orders, although, at the same time, the Church has sought to legitimate discrimination against women priests: draft Priests (Ordination of Women) Measure, s.6. Arguably the Church is protected from action against such discrimination by the Sex Discrimination Act 1975, s.19, although there is some doubt as to whether or not ministers may be said to be employed for any purpose: Re National Insurance Act 1911; Re Employment of Church of England Curates [1911] 2 Ch 563; President of the Methodist Conferences v Parfitt [1984] QB 368 CA. The Church may however be in breach of EC Directive No. 76/207 (Equal Treatment).
80. cf. n.75.
81. Church of England (Miscellaneous Provisions) Measure 1991, ss. 13, 14, 15, which declared that "for the avoidance of doubt" deacons could be appointed as rural deans, and as both residentiary and non-residentiary canons of a cathedral church. There of course the fundamental issue was the possible incapacity of any deacon to hold certain ecclesiastical appointments and in providing that a deacon could hold certain offices the question of gender was effectively sidestepped. Thus there is no difficulty in a woman priest taking office as a rural dean or as a residentiary or non-residentiary canon since all ordained priests have already

been made deacons: Book of Common Prayer, The Ordering of Deacons;
*Canons of the Church of England*, Canon·C3, para 8.
82. Lewis Carroll "*Alice in Wonderland*", chapter 3.

# VIII
# A Slow But Deadly Fuse

## Hugh Craig

This chapter is an attempt to set out the implications of the decision to ordain women to the priesthood for evangelical churchfolk, and especially their laity. The first problem is to define an 'evangelical': for the word is nowadays used so widely as to be almost devoid of meaning: many claiming the title who preach that which their spiritual forefathers denounced. I write as a conservative, or classic, evangelical–one who submits to the 'plain and full meaning'[1] of the 39 Articles: and in particular to Article 6 which places us firmly under the authority of Holy Scripture. To paraphrase Tyndale, we hold that Scripture is for the plough-boy as much as for the priest, and deny that its essential teaching is so obscure that it cannot be discerned without the intermediacy of 'scholars'. We are at home with the scriptural doctrine and stance of the Book of Common Prayer, and see ourselves, with justification, as at the heart of historic Anglicanism however much our detractors wish to represent us as some extreme wing.

Broadly, though not wholly directly, following the Keele Congress in 1967, some evangelicals took a somewhat different turn. The firm doctrinal lines taken by classic evangelicals had denied to many with real ability high office in a church which was (and still is) afraid of real convictions–and some (but by no means all) had in consequence sat light on church structures. At Keele, with some emotion, many decided for the first time to take part in those structures, though subsequent history shows they had no real idea about what to do when they got there. To be an evangelical became 'respectable', and a wider spectrum of people calling themselves by that name appeared. In practice some allowed their distinctive views to be blurred, and in a desire to 'participate' compromised their erstwhile views with those of their more liberal or catholic brethren. Doctrine became less important: Scripture still ruled–but with more relaxed interpretation allowing many to believe that parts of the New Testament were 'culturally conditioned'. Some regard the Book of Common Prayer almost as a relic, and sometimes, perhaps under the influence of the charismatic movement, worship became wholly non-conformist and subjective. Some in practice treat the local church as a kind of religious 'club', and outdoing the congregationalists, treat each as able to make its own rules. Giving labels to groups of people is usually offensive, but to distinguish this very diverse group from the classic evangelicals, let me call them for convenience, (without any unfavourable or favourable over-tones) 'new evangelicals'. It should come as no surprise therefore that in the vote last November 11th., most (but not all) of the 'classic evangelicals' voted against the Measure: most (but not all) of the 'new evangelicals' voted for it.

For most classic evangelicals the issue is basically clear. They may not ignore any passage in the Scriptures. I Cor. 11, I Cor 14, and I Tim. 2. they regard as 'Godbreathed'[2] along with the rest. They are not the easiest of passages. The particular local situations which gave rise to them have to remain a matter of speculation, regardless of the conviction with which some claim their own 'explanation'. Such 'explanations' would be more convincing if they not only identified the 'local application' (which no longer applies) but also the 'abiding principle' which we should still observe. But in practice all too often they empty the passages of all abiding significance. Elsewhere in the New Testament Paul is at pains to stress the essential equality of male and female in our standing before God[3], both being made in the divine image: and much is made of the role of women in the ministry of Christ[4], and in the work of the Church[5]. Yet whatever the local situation in these three passages, Paul enunciates principles (based on the Creation narrative before the Fall) which teach that God is a God of order, and this order extends to His desired relationships between men and women in the worship of the Church. All the New Testament evidence is that the Church eldership was exclusively male: and that to it was primarily reserved authoritative teaching in the local church. Many, because of I Corinthians 11, link this teaching with the parallel 'headship' passage where Paul deals with relationships within marriage[6].

One has to be very careful in using words like 'authoritative' and 'headship' in this matter, lest we read into them sub-Christian concepts. Christ exercised authority, yet submitted to the authority of the Father without in any way being diminished by that fact[7]. Christ's 'headship' over the Church is characterised by the fact that he 'loved it and gave himself for it'[8]: and it was he who warned the disciples about human concepts of authority and said 'it shall *not* be so among you'[9]. And one has to note that the three passages cited are concerned with the divine ordering of the local church's worship. They are not about the ability or superiority of one gender over the other: still less are they about who should be allowed to teach in other circumstances.

There is a problem in identifying New Testament 'eldership' with 'priesthood' in the Church of England: for of recent years we have strayed from the N.T. pattern. In the N.T. eldership was generally plural, and was primarily a pastoral and teaching office. With that it is natural to associate sacramental duties: though the New Testament says almost nothing about the connection. While earlier this century it was normal to speak of the 'ministry of word and sacrament', in more recent years the emphasis has been disproportionately on the sacramental, (the less skilled role, and the less satisfactory in explaining the role of a separate ordained ministry). The Church needs to recover the emphasis of the Prayer Book Ordinal on this point. Yet, for all that, the 'priesthood' of the Church of England is the nearest we have to the N.T. 'elder' and the point at which Paul's teaching is most fittingly applied. Most evangelicals would associate the authority of the priest with the worthy discharge of the office rather than with the office itself. Ideally of course, they should be identical: but even St. Paul found himself in Acts 20. 28-30 in circumstances where he might well have made the same distinction.

If the above is at all a fair statement of classic evangelical views, it follows that for them the practical problem with the Ordination of Women to the Priesthood does not lie, as it does with catholics, in the Holy Communion. Most, perhaps all of them, would note that the New Testament says little on the subject: but would think it only proper that that sacrament should be conducted by the authorised leader of the Church– the elder, or the chief elder–and would therefore find it being done by a woman as at best irregular. (I avoid the word 'President' which many of us find offensive: our Lord presides; the chief minister follows in the steps of Him who said 'I am among you as one that serveth'). But Article 26 'On the unworthiness of ministers that hinders not the effect of the Sacrament' would lead them to class it with lay baptism (irregular, perhaps improper, but not invalid). Some might allow it where there was a mixed team of 'elders' provided it was done under the authority of a 'chief elder' who was male.

As one moves through the spectrum of others who call themselves evangelical the resistance lessens: and one comes to hazier concepts as to the role of the ordained ministry, and even to those who positively advocate lay celebration as a normal piece of church order. (Some classic evangelicals might well also permit lay celebration, but only, and strictly, under emergency conditions–e.g. the 'desert island' scenario, or in case of sudden severe illness of the priest–in strict parallel with the conditions under which lay baptism is accepted).

The more important sticking-point for classic evangelicals comes in relation to authority in the local church. Here the teaching of I Tim. 2 is violated where a woman is given an incumbency with apparent authority over men. That some may be quite capable of exercising that authority, or that some men do it badly, is beside the point: and it ignores whether it is the best use of the woman's talents, or the most effective witness to the unbelieving world. It seems to be a plain contravention of the divine order. Male evangelical clergy will find difficulty if they are expected to work under the authoritiy of a woman colleague. Traditional parishes will find it difficult if they are saddled with a woman incumbent. Now, of course, the legislation permits a parish to refuse such a situation: but life is not as tidy as the legislation assumes. Evangelical laity do not necessarily go to evangelical churches, and the churches to which they do go are not monochrome. So the layman who wishes to remain true to scripture may have real problems in this respect. The temptation will be to go to an eclectic church, and get out of the mainstream of church life, or simply to fall into the besetting sin of the laity, and vote despairingly with one's feet. The majority of new evangelicals, of course, with their less rigorous treatment of the New Testament, will have no such difficulties.

However, in the writer's view, both the above matters are relatively secondary. There are two deeper, more serious and more disruptive issues lurking behind the legislation. The first is the question of marginalisation. In his presidential address to the General Synod last November 12th., Archbishop Carey expressed his determination that following the passing of the Measure steps must be taken to see that the holders of traditional views were not marginalised. That is a worthy sentiment that all will applaud, but to date the advocates of the Measure show absolutely no comprehension as to what its achievement would involve. The recommendation of the House of Bishops this January to appoint three 'flying bishops' to that end is ludicrous in its inadequacy, and is–as far as evangelicals are concerned–dubiously targeted. Even assuming it were the right step, would not 33% of the Church, serviced by 5% of the bishops feel, by that fact alone, that they were being marginalised?

The trouble is far deeper. George Carey wants opponents of women's ordination to have the same chance of being offered a bishopric as others. Good! But does anyone who knows the system of appointing bishops believe that it will actually happen: unless very positive and difficult steps (of which there are no sign) are taken? Will the four members of the Crown Appointments Commission from a diocese that has women priests be really as happy with a traditionalist (even if he will 'work the system') as with a 'liberal'? And even if the appointment of a traditionalist is proposed, has the Archbishop really considered that, on balance, any traditionalist will be proportionately far less likely to accept such an appointment because of the strains it will impose on his conscience? Deep wounds are not that easily healed. George Carey wants traditionalists offering for ordination not to be discriminated against. Good! But how, in practice will it be achieved? Already there are signs that Bishops' selectors, guided by liberally inspired ABM guidelines[10], feel instinctively (and naturally) that a candidate who can accept women's ordination is more likely to 'fit in' than one who cannot. And will young men offer themselves in appropriate numbers, if there is a widespread belief, even now statistically demonstrable (and how much more in the future), that they will consciously or unconsciously be discriminated against in respect of higher office? Unless very strong measures are taken, that have not as yet been publicly disclosed, the Archbishop's good intentions are doomed to failure: and the result will indeed be that the traditionalists will feel themselves—on very solid grounds–to have been marginalised. As I have said in Synod debate,[11] I have never been too worried about those that will leave the Church of England on Day One after the Measure is implemented: but I am greatly worried by those that will have left, voting with their feet, by Year 10. A Church, already in decline, and already all too often alienating its laity as the gulf between laity and leadership widens, that can solemnly contemplate parting with a third of its membership while prating about a decade of evangelism, is a Church with a death wish, or a Church under judgment.

The second major issue is the Church's authority in relation to Scripture. For nearly 20 centuries the most catholic of doctrines has been the authority and inspiration of Scripture–attested to alike by the Reformers or the Council of Trent. Modern Biblical scholarship has chipped away at that authority and in particular has argued that some of the teaching of the New Testament was culturally conditioned in the sense that what was written was not 'Godbreathed', but the reactions of fallible men of limited knowledge to the situation and culture in which they found themselves, and therefore rather less authoritative than the opinion of a modern scholar or bishop, who is freed from the limitations of the first Century. Some (but not all) who have argued for the ordination of women have by some such method explained away I Tim. 2: 'it isn't relevant', 'it doesn't apply to us now', or 'we know better'. But Article 20 on the Authority of the Church wisely reminds us that it 'is not lawful for the Church to ordain anything that is contrary to God's Word written, neither may it so expound one place of Scripture, that it be repugnant to another'. Now the Church of England appears to some of us to have done just that: and taken up a position which effectively makes belief in the cultural conditioning of New Testament writers if not an article of faith, then at least the dominant view, and that at the very time that the House of Bishops felt unable to take an unequivocal line on the Virgin Birth or the Bodily Resurrection of our Lord[12]. This represents an enormous shift in theological emphasis that cannot but be carried into our theological Colleges (it is already there, especially in the diocesan courses), and into our pulpits. And if Paul was culturally conditioned, it is a small (and logical) step to argue that our Lord was also. The Gospel which was given by Christ and the Apostles, becomes a gospel we are free to adapt. The Church of England becomes a sect, and a heretical sect at that. When that becomes evident over the years, the real nature of the decision the Synod took on November 11th will also become apparent. Not because we ordain women, but because of the implications of the way we have chosen to do it, we have lit a slow-burning but deadly fuse. If it is allowed to burn unchecked classic evangelical laity may well be forced to believe both that they are marginalised, and that they have no part in a Church which places its own opinions before the commands of Scripture. In the subsequent re-alignment our 'new evangelical' brethren may find out too late that they have some strange bed-fellows that they have brought into power.

**Notes**

1  Quoted from His Majesty's Declaration, prefacing the Articles.
2  II Tim. 3. 16 : the literal translation of the word Paul coined. The emphasis was not on what happened to the human author–it was on the fact that the Scriptures came from God Himself.
3  e.g. Galatians 3.28.
4  e.g. John 2.5; John 4; Matt. 27.55; Luke 8. 1-3.
5  e.g. Acts 1. 13,14; 18.18,26; 21.9; Rom. 16.1,3.
6  Ephesians 5. 21-32.
7  e.g. John 5. 19-30; I Cor. 15. 24-28; Phil. 2. 5-11.
8  Eph. 5.25
9  Matt. 20.26.
10  ACCM Occasional Paper No. 14 (believed to be under revision).
11  General Synod House of Laity : Report of Proceedings on 11 July 1992: page 9.
12  'The Nature of Christian Belief'. 1986. Church House Publishing.

# IX

# The Wrong Move in the Right Direction?

## *Christine Hall*

It is no easy task to respond to an invitation to identify the implications, for the ministry of women as a whole, of the November 1992 General Synod vote. Certainly it has raised new issues for the Church of England; equally certainly older and unresolved issues seem about to clamour for attention. How some of them will be tackled is perhaps predictable; how others will be handled is yet to be revealed. The outcome will depend on how much effort the Church makes corporately to understand the nature of ministry, both lay and ordained, and how careful it is to explore the whole question of the male/female relationship within the Church and to value the complex variety of life experiences which both unite and differentiate those whom hitherto it has categorised en bloc as 'women'.

## The Nature of Ministry

At the outset of this exploration, it is necessary to identify some basic assumptions and to reflect at some length on the notion that ministry is rooted in the nature of God and in his revelation of himself in Christ. From this flows all that could be said about the specific ministry which women or men might appropriately exercise.

Out of the deepest mystery of his nature, God has revealed himself to us as a unity of three co-equal Persons, Father, Son and Holy Spirit: 'God has no true being apart from communion'. [1] In other words, relationality belongs to his nature in such a way that his very unity is to be understood not as a simple one-ness but as the result of a perfect communion. This notion is deeply rooted in Scripture, particularly but not exclusively in the Gospel of John. [2]

Some of the Greek Fathers of the Church used the term *perichoresis* [3] to describe the divine life of unity-in-communion. The Persons of the Holy Trinity, in giving each other place (as implied in the meaning of the term *perichoresis*), participate in a mutual interchange of love, in which authority, significance and recognition are mutually given and received. As Leonardo Boff has expressed it;

> In our experience of the Mystery, there is indeed diversity (Father, Son and Holy Spirit) and at the same time unity in this diversity, through the communion of the different Persons, by which each is in the others, with the others, through the others and for the others. [4]

An important corollary of this is that human beings, created in the image of God, are most truly themselves, according to the givenness of their nature, when they live in relationship of communion to others and to God, for 'the whole Trinity contains creation in itself. Communion is the first and last word about the mystery of the Trinity.' [5]

Men and women are drawn to participate in the moving dynamic of God's perichoretic life. By the work of the Holy Spirit, who leads us into all truth, the Church is constituted as the Body of the Christ (himself annointed with the same Spirit) and reconciled to the Father. The life of the Holy Trinity can then be seen as the pattern of man's own life. God is truly him in whom we live and move and have our being.

The point has been well made [6] that there is no community designated 'Church' which precedes ministry. The 'variety of gifts' which the Spirit gives for 'all kinds of service' (I Corinthians 12) is not given to a community which already exists and then takes possession of them. Rather there is a simultaneity in the giving of the Spirit's gifts and the constituting of the Church as the Body of Christ, in which all members have a unique place and significance, in relation to each other, a purpose and a role to play for the sake of the common good. If it is indeed the destiny of man, together with the whole creation, to be restored to communion with God and to participation in the life of the Trinity, then the Church's ministry must above all be that through which the very presence and life of the saving Christ is realised.

Once the significance of the ministry is seen to lie in the fact that it is Christ's own ministry, it is easy to understand that it cannot be an object which any of us possesses and can call 'my ministry'. It is not related only to the past, as a reproduction of Christ's service to men and women during his life on earth. Nor is it merely related to the present, on a social service model. It speaks primarily not of the tasks of service we perform, though these may flow from it, but rather of our eternal relation with each other: it has an eschatological dimension. It makes the Church a 'relational reality, a mystery of love, reflecting here and now the very life of the Trinitarian God'. [7]

This view of ministry is not the exclusive property of the Eastern Church. The same understanding lies, for example, behind Henri de Lubac's description of the Church as the sacrament of Christ:

> '...she represents him in the full and ancient meaning of the term; she really makes him present. She not only carries on his work, but she is his very continuation, in a sense far more real than that in which it can be said that any human institution is its founder's continuation.'[8]

This theme is expressed in Vatican II's *Constitution on the Church*, where the Church is described as 'a kind of sacrament of intimate union with God and of the unity of all mankind; that is, she is a sign and an instrument of such union and unity'.[9] It goes without saying that a sacrament is a sign which effects what it signifies.

The Church's sacraments are, to use de Lubac's phrase, 'intrinsically social'. [10] The setting in which the initiated Christian is given place, in the perichoretic sense, is the Eucharist, the assembly of the people of God, where the Church becomes what it is. The ministry which rests on the mark of baptism and the sacred ministry which rests on the mark of ordination are seen there clearly in their different ways, as Christ's own ministry of service, sacrifice and reconciliation, whose purpose is the restoration of communion between man and God. Faith, as the way we understand our ultimate destiny to be communion with God, and order, as the way consequently we organise ourselves and express our relation to each other in the context of that communion, are there revealed in their true inseparability.

It seems unlikely that the Church of England will be prepared to question, still less discard, its social service, task- and function-orientated models of ministry for lay and ordained, in order to express itself consciously as a Church, whose essence is communion and whose goal is participation in the divine life. From its cultural context, it is individualistically orientated and conditioned to understand more readily what its members 'do' than what they 'are' in the vast complex of ministerial relationships within the Church itself and in the Church's relating to the world.

## Women's Ministry

A word needs to be said about the phrase 'women's ministry'. The complementary phrase, 'men's ministry' is not in use, which would seem to indicate two things. First, men are not considered to be such a monochrome group that anything said about the ministry of one of them might reasonably be said about the ministry of all of them collectively. Rather they are differentiated. Secondly, men's ministry is acceptable and unquestioned, even normative, whilst women's ministry is a notion which carries an air of uncertainty, hence the use of the phrase and its concomitant failure to accord personal distinctiveness to women.

In baptism, the sacrament which confers the mandate for ministry, there is 'no more distinction between male and female, for all of you are one in Christ Jesus' (Gal. 3:27-28). Whilst in some cultures at some times it may be customary for men and women to exercise ministry in specifically different ways, these are only the outward forms not to be confused with the charisms of the Holy Spirit which they express. Outward forms may change. That many women have, for example, beautified countless churches by arranging flowers does not mean either that in today's world they should be ashamed of that gift, if they have it, or be confined to that particular activity, if they have other skills to be used for the good of the whole.

At different times in Christian history, women have enjoyed different degrees of freedom and equality of value in the Church. It is nevertheless true that,

> 'in history and actuality, the difference and complementarity of the male/female relationship is distorted by sin into the dominance of male over female and the oppression of women by men. This distortion of the order of creation is redeemed by the sacrifice of Christ and represented in the Church's life.'[11]

The question is, 'To what extent can the rectification of this distortion truly be seen to be represented in the life of the Church?' There is considerable confusion in the Church of England about the difference between ministry and order, that is between the ministry of all the baptised and the ordained ministry. The confusion is compounded because many people refer to ordained ministry as 'the ministry' and speak of 'going into the ministry', which implies that those who are not ordained are not involved in ministry. The nature and relationship between ministry (in which the whole people of God is involved on the basis of baptism) and ordained ministry (in which bishops, deacons and priests are the visible image of what is true of the Church as a whole) is in urgent need of clarification.[12]

In addition, like other human beings, Christians have difficulty in differentiating between one object or person and another, without at the same time apportioning value. Church life reflects the conviction held by many people that ordained ministry is 'better' than lay ministry, and priesthood is 'higher' than diaconate. To this point of view, the vote in support of the ordination of women to the priesthood signals the fact that women 'have made it'. Regrettably, it may also make it possible for the Church to go on neglecting to face and deal with the distortion of the male/female relationship, on the grounds that women (not just some women, but all women) have now 'got what they wanted'. The result of this may well be that no further effort will be made to accord personal distinctiveness in ministry to lay women. At the same time, it seems unlikely that women admitted to priesthood will find their position much better than it was before. Their new place will not necessarily guarantee that they will be better valued, recognised for all they have to offer, given more responsibility or a greater share in decision-making. It has been found repeatedly in professions and organisations which have been dominated by men, that women do not have a real opportunity to reach the higher levels, unless a policy of positive discrimination is applied.

## The Unexpressed Side of *Perichoresis*

'...the heart of *perichoresis*, of that to and fro of love, is the giving of authority and the receiving of authority from each other. Authority is not the same as power; it is the spontaneous flow of truth coming out of the creative centre of an author. The essence of the Trinity is not a power-sharing but a self-emptying through which they recognise and set free the truth in each other, so the three become one. This self-emptying for others is the agape of God ('greater love has no one').'[13]

The above statement, if in any way it approximates to the reality of the divine life, must call into question the way in which the Gospel is embodied within the visible structures of the Church. The context under consideration here is not that wide context of the ministry of all the baptised but the specific context of the relationality within the ordained ministry. As a result of the November 1992 vote, women will be admitted to a visible structure of priestly ministry which seems in itself to be in need of change. This structure has all the appearances of a system of 'power-sharing', a competitive career structure, which gives too little acknowledgement to the relational nature of ministry, a structure in which the priestly figure is still too often a 'sole performer', expected to be omnicompetent, making or shaping all the vital decisions and carrying out most of them.

It is hard to locate any really consistent pattern of that 'to and fro' of the divine perichoresis, rooted in an authority which is not power, in communion not individuality, in mutual recognition not competition. If the Church is indeed the sacrament of Christ, who is in turn the sacrament of God[14], should that pattern not be found in the relations between the orders of bishop, priest and deacon? In their liturgical and pastoral life, should there not be a visible embodiment of the perichoretic activity of God?

One particular point which will be important for our exploration later on is that, as a result of the incarnation, perichoresis involves also the self-emptying of the Son of God (Phil. 2:6-11), who learned obedience by the things he suffered, and submitted himself humbly to the Father for the sake of the salvation of the world (Heb. 5: 7-8). It is this which seems most noticeably absent from the life of the Church, for it cannot flourish in the presence of domination and competition. Like authority, obedience and submission have taken on distorted meanings and have become unpopular concepts. Should it not be possible however, in the Body of Christ to see the clear image of his, 'self-emptying for others' which is an indication of the 'agape of God'?

Soon after the vote, feminist and not-so-feminist thinkers began to suggest that the admission of women to the priesthood in the Church of England would be nothing more than a patronising pat on the head from the male establishment, implying only a slight degree of recognition. It would mean, they argued, collusion by women in a system which in itself was designed to exclude them from any real participation and which would continue to deny them access to its inner life and decision making.

The grounds for holding this view are sadly quite compelling. Across the whole spectrum of churchmanship ordained women who have been in the diaconate for the last five years tell of difficulties in being accepted on terms of equal value. Their collected experiences of non-acceptance, and of negative attitudes towards them may well indicate that the Church of England already has serious gender-based problems. In society as a whole, women live in the context of violence towards them in many areas of their lives. There is a real need to ensure that the ministerial priesthood embodies the Christ who represented human nature to the Father by his self-emptying and his sacrifice. It seems clear that we know too little about how men and women are meant to relate to each other in the order of redemption. In fact we may know so little that to admit women to the priesthood without exploring the current attitudes towards them in much greater depth would be a not inconsiderable risk.

The Church needs to consider the whole area of male/female relationships seriously and theologically. The implications of its not doing so are that women as priests will continue to operate (as women still do for the most part in secular employment[15]) in auxiliary capacities. All too often they will find themselves working under the direction of men who are less able than they are, or in positions which do scant justice to their skills and gifts. Without necessarily wishing it, large numbers of them are likely to be deployed in part-time or non-stipendiary ministry[16]. Increasingly those who succeed in moving to posts 'higher up' the existing career structure will be expected to 'fit in' to a structure designed for men, which does not take into account the specific insights and styles which are characteristic of women.

Will there be a continuing pressure on women to 'fit in' to existing structures as they struggle for preferment? Or will a definite effort be made to bring forward a generation of women to assume leadership roles, and to ensure that the perceptions and modes of operation they bring with them will be incorporated into the existing structures? Will anything be modified to accommodate them?

The likelihood is that some women at least will be themselves and will not necessarily behave according to men's expectation. The reaction of the system may be to try to confine them to areas where they can have little influence. Such a tendency would be given impetus and encouragement by the legislation itself, because, for the first time in the history of the Church, the legal right will be given to any member of the people of God, ordained or lay, to object, on grounds of gender, to those whom bishops have ordained to the priesthood.[17]

It seems unlikely that, in the ensuing situation, anything will be able to be done to re-express the Gospel notions of self-emptying, obedience and submission, which, together with a proper theological understanding of authority, have been suppressed in the Church's embodiment of the *perichoresis* of the Holy Trinity.

It may well be of crucial importance that women play a leading role in the recovery of self-emptying service, submission and obedience within the corporate life of the Church. There is no suggestion that women should adopt (or re-adopt) the passive, submissive and secondary role they were traditionally expected to occupy, nor is there any reason that they should be wholly defined by their biological functions. At the same time, there is evidence from psychological research to suggest that what remains unexpressed in the life of the Church has in fact been suppressed, for particular reasons, in every area of human life.

Some psychologists believe that women have been made 'carriers' for society of certain aspects of the total human experience whose value has been denied by the male dominant group.[18] The rejected parts of experience do not fit with the values normally involved in male development in which generally there is an emphasis on mastering weakness, denying vulnerability, cultivating strength, self-sufficiency, competence, and independence, going it alone and winning. The unwanted aspects of experience have in fact endowed women with an abundance of qualities which make them skilled at fostering corporate life, living beyond themselves and participating in the growth of others. They are able to give without experiencing a sense of loss; their idea of development does not involve the process of separating competitively from others, and they understand the significance of relationality.[19] It is not difficult to see that the experiences women 'carry' closely resemble those aspects of the self-emptying of the Son of God which seem to be poorly expressed in the Church's life.

In present circumstances the task of restoring the full perichoretic pattern cannot be done from the perspective of priesthood. The priest, eucharistically and in so many other ways, has become accustomed to going it alone, and no doubt many will continue to do so. In the present situation, the priest is not obviously a positive symbol of relationality. However, the deacon is.

## The Need for a Permanent Diaconate

For some people, one of the implications of the vote to permit the ordination of women to the priesthood may be that there is, in the first place, no further need for a permanent diaconate. It could be argued that it has served its purpose as a means to an end. Secondly, as the Church of England reviews its financial position, it may be tempted to continue with its customary assumptions that there is a shortage of priests and that deacons are less 'useful' than priests because they are not, as some have remarked, 'a eucharistic pair of hands'. There seems to be a significant number of women deacons and ordinands indicating that they have no wish to be ordained to the priesthood. Some have expressed the fear that they will be told that to receive or continue to receive a salary from the Church, they will have to be priests. Thirdly, the Church may continue to regard the diaconate as an order defined by tasks and functions, with its rationale in the detail of its social involvement rather than in its relationship to the perichoretic life of God.

As an order whose primary raison d'être is to represent Christ in his servanthood ('I am among you as one who serves'), the diaconate is the order which is most easily able to counterbalance any overemphasis on power. It is arguably the radical position from which it would be possible to restore to the Church the hidden and rejected parts of perichoresis (self-emptying, obedience, submission). It is appropriate that the diaconate should be the order which expresses these. The deacon's liturgical actions already make it quite clear that this is not an order which lives for itself.

> 'They (deacons) are witnesses to a very different world order, in which Christ himself is among us as 'one who serves', and where ambition is turned on its head: 'whoever would be first among you must be the willing slave of all' (Mark 10: 44). In the context in which Jesus was speaking, the slave, legally, was not a human person with rights: the value of his life was determined simply in terms of its value for others.'[20]

The deacon is a necessary and invaluable participant in *perichoresis*. The deacon cannot be a sole performer but 'manifestly needs someone else'[21]. The deacon is a channel of Christ's enabling ministry so that the whole people of God may become what they are already, the servant Church. When the 'leader becomes as one who serves' (Luke 22:25-27), this 'reversal of the normal human pattern of relationships is the sign of the dawning of the new age of the Kingdom of God'.[22]

It is not suggested that all deacons should be female. There is
no reason why men should not be able to re-embody what has
been suppressed. The point is that deacons involuntarily embody self-emptying and authority-as-service, simply because it is
in the nature of their order to do so. If they are not present in
the life of the Church, this essential image is lacking. It is greatly
to be hoped that the Church will see the implications of this and
that the November 1992 vote will not be regarded as the end of
the permanent diaconate.

## The wrong move in the right direction?

Twenty years may seem a long time, and it is almost twenty
years since the General Synod declared that there was no
fundamental objection to the ordination of women to the priesthood. Yet, in the historical perspective, the questions which
arise out of the relationship of women to men are new questions
for the Church.

A volume of papers on various aspects of women's ministry
was prepared in 1919 for the Lambeth Conference[23], at about
the same time as women received their political rights. During
World War II, women's role in society was seen to have been
damagingly conditioned by unchallenged assumptions about
them. Since then, psychology has raised many questions about
the differentiation between women and men, but it is still by no
means clear how differentiation of gender impinges on religious,
political and personal life.

It is evident that men and women are not interchangeable,
and for the Church it should also be evident that the place given
to them should be in conformity with the given differentiation of
their created nature, not at variance with it.

The most serious implications of the vote for the ministry of
women in the Church of England are:

> that a sense that finally women have been given their
> just reward, will impede a real examination of the con-

tention (re-iterated by Brian Horne among others) that 'the male/female relationship is distorted by sin into the dominance of male over female';

that no further attempt will be made to work out whether or not there is a specific, gender-based women's ministry at all;

that nothing will be done to accommodate women into the existing priestly structures, but that they will be required to conform to male ways of operating or to take posts for which there is the least competition with men;

that it will be presumed that there is no further need for a permanent diaconate.

Ordaining women to the priesthood will not be the same as giving full recognition and place to their gifts, though the Church needs to move in the direction of giving that recognition. *A Fearful Symmetry?* posed a number of questions.

'Is it providential that there are divisions within the Church, so that one group may move forward while the others watch? Will the rest of Christendom learn from the Anglicans' mistakes? Will Anglicans make the wrong move in the right direction? More fundamentally, is it possible at the present time, that some groups of Christians may be called to act on behalf of others? Are there complementary roles given to our Churches in their present state of partial and imperfect communion? Can we support and help one another even when we do not wholly agree with one another? But such things have to be born and grow out of a common mind between the Churches, and cannot be achieved by unilateral action.'[24]

**Notes**
1. J. Zizioulas, *Being as Communion* (DLT 1985), pp.15-19.
2. See John 5: 19-22, 16: 13, 17: 21-22.

3. Peri = around. Chora = place. See Allchin et al, *A Fearful Symmetry?* (SPCK 1992), pp.28-32, for a discussion of the meaning of *perichoresis* in the context of the complementarity of men and women in ministry.

4. L. Boff, *Trinity and Society* (Burns & Oates 1988), p.3.

5. Boff, p.16.

6. Among others, by J. Zizioulas in *Being as Communion*.

7. Zizioulas, p.220.

8. H. de Lubac, *Catholicism* (Burns & Oates 1950), quoted in Avery Dulles, *Models of the Church* (Gill & MacMillan 1988), p. 63.

9. Dogmatic Constitution of the Church, Chapter I, art. 1.

10. In Dulles, p.67.

11. See Brian Horne, Theses, no. 9. From 22 Theses on Christianity and Gender; (unpublished,London, 1992)

12. For a discussion on the relationship between the ordained ministry and the Church as a whole, see R. Hannaford, *Towards a Theology of the Diaconate*, in C. Hall (Ed.), *The Deacon's Ministry* (Gracewing 1991), pp.25-43.

13. Allchin et. al., *A Fearful Symmetry?*, p.28.

14. de Lubac, in Dulles, p.63.

15. According to the Equal Opportunities Commission, women earn 22% less than men and 'frequently have no option but to work far below their capacity and their qualification level'. They 'still encounter patronising attitudes' and 'lack of recognition'. EOC, *The Equality Agenda*.

16. A large percentage of women ordinands currently receive training on part-time courses, which many complete whilst simultaneously holding a full-time job. This means that they do not have the opportunity to take degrees in Theology, as their counterparts in Theological Colleges do. This in turn prevents their development as theological educators and limits their prospects of service to the Church.

17. See Draft Priests (Ordination of Women) Measure, Part II, *Discharge of Functions*.

18. See Professor Jean Baker Miller, *Toward a New Psychology of Women* (Pelican 1988).

19. Miller, passim.

20. J. Pinnock, *History of the Diaconate*, in C. Hall (Ed.) *The Deacon's Ministry*, (Gracewing 1991), pp.9-10.

21. See Antonia Lynn, *Finding Images*, in *The Deacon's Ministry*, pp.106-107.

22. R. Hannaford, in *The Deacon's Ministry*, p.33.

23. *The Ministry of Women*, SPCK 1919.

24. Allchin et. al. p.54.

# X
# Alternative Episcopal Oversight: A Legal View

## John Rees

## Introduction

This paper addresses the legal issues arising from 'alternative episcopal oversight'.

The Archbishops' Commission on the Ecclesiastical Courts in 1954 emphasised that "a Bishop's relationship with both his clergy and his laity today is predominantly a pastoral one . . . . first and foremost [he is] a pastor rather than a judge"[1]. Whilst inevitably this paper is bound to focus on the juridical structure within which such pastoral concern may operate, it should be borne in mind that part of the strength of the Church of England is its ability to look beyond the strict letter of the law, and to try to find pastoral solutions to problems which may appear legally intractable.

At the Reformation, the Church of England continued the tradition of territorial episcopal oversight which had developed in Western Christendom. In its Ordinal, it robustly stated that "from the Apostles' time there have been these Orders of Ministers in Christ's church: Bishops, Priests and Deacons"[2]. It puts great store by its claim to historical continuity within the

Catholic tradition, and understands that each of its Bishops "truly and effectively symbolises the relation of himself, and all those with whom he is bound in his Diocese, with the church through the ages back to the time of the early Church"[3].

## The Parish the Diocese and the Bishop

Parishioners and congregations tend to think of the parish as the essential building block of the Church of England. However, legally that is not the case: the primary unit is the Diocese. The underlying principle is *ubi episcopus, ibi ecclesia*. Hooker aptly described the bishops of the Church of England as "bishops with restraint... whose regiment over the Church is contained within some definite, local compass, beyond which compass their jurisdiction reacheth not"[4]. The diocese provides the geographical boundaries of its Bishop's authority.

Within the boundaries of each diocese, with some minor exceptions[5], the bishop is "the chief pastor... [and] father in God"[6]. His is the cure of souls throughout the diocese, as its principal minister[7] or 'incumbent paramount'[8]. He has full superintendence of its parishes, save in so far as he may have delegated to others; and he is entitled to visit any or all of the parishes from time to time "to the end that he may get some good knowledge of the state, sufficiency and ability" of those engaged in the church's ministry in them[9]. He is charged with administering appropriate discipline throughout his Diocese in accordance with the law of the land[10].

Subject to the exceptions we have noted, no minister (including a bishop of any other diocese or Province), may exercise his ministry within the bishop's diocese unless he holds his licence or written permission to do so. In the last resort, a bishop could take legal proceedings to prevent such unauthorised ministry within his diocese[11].

Whilst both the polity and the liturgy of the Church of England now emphasise the role played by the whole body of the church in the appointment of its bishops[12], its insistence on historical continuity marks the Church of England off clearly from Reformed churches with an episcopal structure but whose bishops derive their authority entirely 'from below', by election or appointment deriving ultimately from the consent of its membership. By contrast, the authority of a bishop in the Church of England is understood as deriving 'from above', by participation in the Apostolic Succession. There is more to the authority of a bishop of the Church of England than can be explained by the voluntary submission of clergy and their people to him.

In addition to diocesan bishops, the Church of England is familiar with the concept of suffragan bishops, and indeed there has been a vast growth in their numbers during the present century[13]. Suffragans operate by delegation or commission from their diocesan bishop, and their authority derives from him to carry out such tasks as he may delegate to them[14]. There is also provision for permanent delegation to 'area bishops' under the Dioceses Measure 1978, whereby the delegation continues notwithstanding a change of diocesan bishop; but the principle remains the same, namely that the authority which is being exercised by the suffragan or area bishop ultimately derives from the bishop of the diocese.

Still other bishops may hold office within the diocese as assistants, these generally being retired bishops or former bishops of overseas dioceses (though it is possible for a bishop of a non-Anglican communion whose orders are recognised by the Church of England to assist[15]). Again, however, the principle remains that such assistants derive the authority for their ministry in the diocese from the bishop of the diocese who has invited or authorised them to assist.

However, the Church of England has no recent acquaintance with, or legal provision for, types of episcopate familiar to the ancient and mediaeval church, such as *chorepiscopi* ('country bishops'), bishops *in partibus infidelium* or co-adjutor bishops[16]. In particular, the concept of the bishop 'at large' is quite unknown to it[17].

## The Clergy and their Bishop

Upon ordination and licensing, the clergy of the Church of England are required to take an oath of obedience to the bishop of the diocese in which they are being ordained or licensed. In it, they confirm that they will obey their bishop "in all things lawful and honest"[18]. At the heart of the present crisis in the Church of England is a conviction on the part of some clergy that the authority of their bishops, both to provide full and sacramental oversight, and to require their obedience, has been compromised by the General Synod's decision to ordain women. This step is seen by them as having been taken *ultra vires*, as a purported exercise of a legislative authority in the matter of sacramental ministry which the Church of England simply does not possess, and an affront to its Catholic and Biblical integrity.

In consequence, it is said by such clergy that they will be "out of communion" with their Bishops. For some, the only response to this must be to find another Christian community whose Catholic or Biblical integrity they consider free of doubt. Others have indicated that they could remain within the sacramental life of the Church of England if they could avail themselves of some alternative structure of episcopal oversight. To satisfy their concerns, this oversight would have to be provided by Bishops whose authority they consider unimpeachable.

The Bishops of the Provinces of Canterbury and York, meeting in Manchester in January 1993, drew up an outline for a scheme of episcopal oversight which might serve to resolve the difficulty. As a pastoral solution, it has great merit: it offers an episcopal point of reference for those clergy who feel they cannot accept the direct ministry of their diocesan bishop. However, the reservations expressed by the clergy themselves, and the pastoral suggestion put forward to meet it, both deserve further analysis from a legal point of view.

## A Reflection on the question of Communion

From a purely juridical point of view, the position is clear. There may be theological arguments against the involvement of the secular authorities in the affairs of the Church of England, but the fact remains that its constitution is part of the law of the land; so long as it exercises its legal powers constitutionally, its decisions will be upheld by the courts[19]. Whilst there may be a strong ecumenical case for saying that the Church of England ought not to act unilaterally in altering its pattern of ministry in the way that it has done[20], consultation or agreement with the wider Church is not a legal requirement for the Established Church in England.

The authority of the Church of England to legislate for itself is then beyond dispute *as a matter of law*. It follows that once the new Measure has received the Royal Assent, and the amending canons have been promulged under it, acts done in pursuance of the legislation will be recognised as valid according to law. It will make no difference to their legal validity that some members of the Church of England are unable to recognise or receive them *for theological reasons*. So far as the law is concerned, no cause of action would arise from any alleged 'breach of communion'. In consequence, there is no legal reason why it should be necessary to provide any alternative scheme of episcopal oversight.

However, there are powerful pastoral reasons why some alternative provision seems necessary. Clergy and parishioners do feel themselves dispossessed, and the bishops are concerned to make provision for them whilst at the same time giving full weight to the General Synod's decision to proceed with the ordination of women to the priesthood. Before turning to consider the legal effects of the proposed scheme of alternative oversight, it is worth examining more closely the precise need which it is intended to meet.

This is not as easy a task as it might at first seem: for example, in its January statement, the council of 'Forward in Faith', variously described the impairment of communion as arising from promulgation of the new canons, from the fact of a given bishop ordaining a woman as a priest, or from a bishop endorsing the ministry of a woman priest[21]. There seem to be a number of different criteria which might be applied in determining whether a breach of communion has taken place. We may consider several possibilities.

The clearest case would be that of a bishop who had voted for the legislation, and had then himself acted under it to ordain a woman as a priest. Those who regard the Church as having no authority (save in civil law) to introduce this alteration to the pattern of Catholic order would be bound to consider their communion with such a bishop as being, at the very least, impaired.

It is less easy to see how they would regard, say, a bishop who had voted *for* the legislation but had then decided that it would be imprudent to ordain any woman as a priest (or during any interval between the date when the legislation comes into effect and the date upon which he first ordains a suitable woman candidate as a priest). Would communion with him be impaired simply by the views he was known to hold, or only by his acting upon those views in pursuance of the legislation he had approved?

Similarly, how would a bishop be regarded who permitted his suffragans to ordain women whilst himself refraining from doing so[22]. Would it make any difference if he had himself voted *against* the legislation, but had not followed this up by making the declaration against permitting women to minister as priests within his diocese?

The most thorough-going approach would, of course, see the breach of communion as flowing from the simple fact of the legislation being passed: this approach is touched on in 'Forward in Faith's' statement, but it is hard to see how any person putting this interpretation upon the difficulty could regard himself as being in communion with any bishop who continued in the ministry of the Church of England as by law established, whatever view that bishop had taken in the debates, and whatever steps he took to distance himself from the implementation of the legislation. The continuance of such a bishop in collegiality with bishops who had consented to, or acted upon, legislation perceived as being in breach of the wider Church's authoritative teaching would be bound to impugn that bishop's own authority.

There is more to this than legal hair-splitting: depending upon the assessment made in each case, different solutions by way of alternative episcopal oversight may be necessary; this is particularly the case since, as we shall see in the next section, the oversight supplied by the proposed scheme will derive its authority, in the absence of specific legislation, from the diocesan bishop himself[23]. If the Church of England is to continue with an episcopate whose authority ultimately derives 'from above' rather than 'from below', then it is important that any scheme intended to meet the assertion of broken communion does address precisely the act which is considered to have done the damage: without agreed criteria, we are left with an episcopate that depends for its authority ultimately on individual assessment of whether or not communion exists.

## A Reflection on the Proposed Scheme

Since, as we have seen, from a strictly legal point of view there is no case to answer, the solution to the pastoral problem ought not to give rise to any particular legal difficulty. Ironically, however, things are not so simple.

As we noted at the outset, the basis of episcopal oversight in the Church of England is territorial. Our bishops are bishops "with restraint", in Hooker's words[24]. A bishop of the Church of England cannot exercise his ministry in the diocese of another bishop without the latter's authority to do so. Conversely, he is not subject to the intrusion of another bishop into his own diocese without his consent.

This has obvious significance for any scheme of alternative oversight: any bishop designated to provide episcopal oversight for those who feel unable to accept the jurisdiction of their own bishop can only operate within the latter's diocese with his consent and therefore in the final analysis under his authority. This is explicitly acknowledged in the Bishops' proposals[25]. The arrangement depends entirely upon the voluntary co-operation of all concerned[26]. In the absence of goodwill and co-operation, a further change in the law would be required, to alter the traditional territorial basis of episcopal oversight[27].

However, just as we have seen that the alleged impairment of communion itself is not strictly a legal problem, so it may be that a solution can be found short of coercive legislation to deal with the intractable obstacles that arise from applying strictly territorial principles.

The Church of England is already familiar with effective pastoral and episcopal structures that cannot be fully explained in legal terms. We have noted, for example, the customary exemption of certain college chapels from the jurisdiction of the bishop of the diocese in which they are situated. Even though that is the case in strict law, as a matter of practice, many of the college chaplains working in such 'extra-diocesan' places nevertheless hold the licence of the diocesan bishop in order that they may play a full part in the life of the surrounding diocese; they value their participation in it, assisting the diocesan clergy in ministry, particularly during the vacations, and find support and enrichment through their fellowship with the neighbouring chapter of clergy.

By contrast, prison chaplains, who by law *are* under the authority of the diocesan bishop of the diocese in which their institution is located [28] also belong to an informal structure of ministry within the prison service, with a Bishop for Prisons at its head. This bishop is designated as such by the Archbishop of Canterbury, whose legal authority for making such provision is far from obvious. Nevertheless, the Bishop for Prisons' episcopal ministry is appreciated and pastorally effective, notwithstanding the absence of any formal legal foundation underpinning it.

From a legal point of view, still more problematical is the

position of military chaplains. They are appointed by the Ministry of Defence, and are licensed directly by the Archbishop of Canterbury, whether they are to serve in the Diocese of Canterbury, elsewhere in the Province of Canterbury, in the province of York, or elsewhere in Scotland, Wales, Northern Ireland or on service for Her Majesty the Queen around the world. The service chaplains and garrison congregations enjoy a parallel structure within the Church of England, under a 'Bishop to the Forces' appointed by the Archbishop of Canterbury; and the Chaplain to the Fleet,the Chaplain-General, and the Chaplain-in-Chief to the Royal Air Force each hold the title of Archdeacon. Whilst the legal basis for this arrangement may be far from clear[29], there is no doubt about its pastoral effectiveness, and about the importance of the service chaplains and congregations within the life of the Church of England.

These apparently anomalous arrangements do suggest that the Church of England can develop within itself structures that do justice to perceived pastoral need even though they might not fit neatly into a consistent legal pattern. It would not be unreasonable to think that the Bishops' proposal for extended episcopal care may find acceptance in the life of the Church of England in just the same way.

## Conclusion

To sum up, once the new Measure and canons have passed into law, whatever theological reservations any particular clergyman or parishioner may have, there is no legal basis for asserting that any impairment of communion has taken place. The Church of England will simply have changed its law, as it is entitled by law to do.

Such theological reservations as there are, will, however, have given rise to a pastoral need which the bishops are concerned to meet. The scheme of extended episcopal care presently proposed by the bishops envisages a voluntary arrangement whereby some bishops, perceived as having an impaired relationship with their clergy or parishioners, will authorise other bishops not so regarded to minister on their behalf in their dioceses.

It is by no means obvious that the arrangement *will* meet the needs of all those who feel themselves prejudiced by the General Synod's decision to ordain women as priests, but then, it is unlikely that *any* scheme of alternative oversight could meet the variety of perceived need. The scheme offered by the Bishops fits into a tradition of pastoral response characteristic of the Church of England: for some, that will be seen as its great weakness; for others, as one of its strengths.

### Notes

1. *Report of the Archbishops' Commission on Ecclesiastical Courts* (SPCK 1954) p51
2. The late Chancellor Garth Moore commented that this statement had been made "optimistically", *Canon Law*, (1st ed. OUP 1967) p122
3. *Episcopal Ministry*, Report by the Archbishops' Group on the Episcopate, (Church House Publishing, 1990). Phillimore in the Preface to the first edition of his *Ecclesiastical Law* described it as "that great branch of the Catholic Church, called the English Church"
4. Hooker, *Laws of Ecclesiastical Polity*, VII, ii, 2
5. There are in a number of dioceses 'peculiars', and extra-diocesan places, chapels or buildings which are conventionally regarded as falling outside the bishop's jurisdiction (college chapels in Oxford and Cambridge provide cases in point)
6. Canon C 18.4
7. Burn's *Ecclesiastical Law* (2nd ed., London 1767) describes the bishop as "the universal minister...overseer and superintendent; so called from that watchfulness, care, charge and faithfulness which by his place and dignity he hath and oweth to the church"
8. Moore, op.cit., p.18
9. Canon C 18.4
10. Canon C 18.7; the method of discipline would as so far as any legal proceedings are concerned, follow principally the statutory provisions contained in the Ecclesiastical Jurisdiction Measure 1963 (as amended)
11. Canon C8
12. See, for example, the recent article in the *Church Times* (31 December 1992) by the Archbishops' Appointments Secretary, explaining the working of the Crown Appointments Commission; and paragraph 12 of the *Alternative Service Book 1980*, Order for Ordination or Consecration of a Bishop
13. For figures, see *Episcopal Ministry*, pp.180 *et seqq*; the Commission notes that "the province of Canterbury and York are alone within the Anglican Communion in having more suffragans than diocesans. This is a clear case of response to a felt

and expressed pastoral need".

14. See Suffragan Bishops Act 1534, and Dioceses Measure 1978, s.10
15. Overseas and other Clergy Measure 1967, s.4
16. See Phillimore, *Ecclesiastical Law*, (2n ed., Sweet & Maxwell, 1895), chapter II; and *Episcopal Ministry*, pp. 181- 183
17. See Hooker, *loc-cit*
18. Canon C 14.3
19. See, for example, the recent case of *Brown and others v Archbishops of Canterbury and York*, reported in *Times*, 26 June 1990 (Hoffman, J.), and 20 February 1991 (Court of Appeal). Leave to appeal to the House of Lords was refused by the Court of Appeal, and the Lords rejected a petition for leave to do so.
20. The arguments are powerfully stated in J. Halliburton, *The Authority of a Bishop*, (SPCK, 1988), Excursus II; wider consultation, at least within the Anglican Communion, was one of the purposes underlying the Lambeth Conference discussions in 1988, and the Eames Commission Report in 1989, though both were addressed primarily to the issue of women *in the episcopate*
21. See Statement issued by 'Forward in Faith' (*Church Times 23 January 1993*)
22. "If a diocesan who was opposed to the ordination of women himself refrained from ordaining women but allowed his suffragan to do so, could it not be argued that within the episcopal college of the diocese itself there was reflected the diversity of view and practice within the Church of England as a whole" (report of several Northern Bishops meeting on 13 June 1991–'the Ripon proposals').
23. The Bishops' Manchester Statement emphasises that "each diocesan bishop will continue to accept full responsibility for the episcopal oversight and pastoral care of all in his charge". They speak carefully of episcopal oversight being *extended* under the proposed scheme. It is not strictly a scheme for *alternative* oversight.
24. See note 2 above
25. See note 21 above.
26. The Bishops do acknowledge that their proposals "might involve synodical action," but this appears to be a reference to the creation of new posts (the so-called 'flying bishops') certainly, further legislation would be necessary to create any episcopal appointments whose sole purpose was to provide "extended care".
27. This may be the kind of legislation the Bishop of London had in mind in his first public reponse to the Bishops' Statement (see *Church Times*, 22 January 1993). He indicated that, "people will need to be assured of something more than a grace-and-favour arrangement, some sort of institutional element".
28. Extra-Parochial Ministry Measure 1967, s.2
29. It is probably based on custom, as least so far as the Royal Navy is concerned; the Army Chaplains Act 1868 has never been formally implemented, and is thought to be incapable of implementation; licences appear to be authorised by exercise of the Royal Prerogative, under a Warrant of 1928; when the matter came before the General Synod for consideration some years ago it was agreed that matters should be left as they stood.

# XI

# The Manchester Statement [1]
# – A Comment

## *Michael Watts*

This Statement was awaited eagerly by many, impatiently by some. It promised to reveal the first-fruits of that period of calm reflection for which the Archbishop of Canterbury had appealed in the immediate wake of the vote in the General Synod on November 11th 1992, an appeal which was re-echoed by the Bishop of Chichester and others in their statement on November 17th. That two month interlude was characterised by public restraint on both sides in the debate. The Movement for the Ordination of Women did not rejoice: the Forward in Faith Movement, rightly assessing the mood of uncertainty in the Church, was given a low-key launch. Both sides were helped to an inescapable awareness of the seriousness of the situation for which neither proponents or opponents appeared to be prepared, by reports of the sympathetic response to the pastoral needs of marginalised Anglicans by the Roman Hierarchy in this country. This could not have been anticipated. Slowly, during the two months that elapsed between the Synod's vote and the meeting of the House of Bishops in the Parker Hotel, Manchester, the possibility of decisive schism within the Church of England began to sink in, albeit a schism which, as Cardinal Hume was to suggest later, within the providence of God might contribute to the unity of the Church.[2] Many, myself included, observed Christmas in their parish churches in 1992 wondering if it was to be for the last time as members of the Church of England.

When the Bishops' Statement was issued on January 14th there was a significant number of people, both lay and ordained, who were looking to the Bishops to provide a way for them to remain with integrity as members of the Church of England after the promulgation of the Canon to make it lawful for women to be ordained to the Priesthood. They were bitterly disappointed. They had asked for bread and were offered what had all the appearance of a stone. At first many found the heavily-emphasised unanimity of the Bishops' Statement difficult to understand as they recalled that the House included those Bishops who had opposed the motion in the General Synod on November 11th. The sense of perplexity arose, in part, from false expectations of what could be achieved. Reflection showed that they had not compromised their position by assenting to these proposals. They were free still to issue the necessary declaration forbidding the ordination of women to the priesthood in their dioceses. Nothing had changed that. The House of Bishops meeting in Manchester was addressing the needs of those opposing laypeople and priests who would find themselves in dioceses where no declaration against the ordination of women would be issued and those dioceses in which, for a time, such a declaration might be issued but not renewed subsequently.

Probably the opponents of the Measure in the House of Bishops achieved as much as was possible at that time, within the limits of what was legally possible and the reported intransigence of some of the other members of that House. The need to provide safeguards had long been recognised.[3] Whether many Bishops empathise with those who find themselves obliged to oppose the Measure is open to question.

Re-reading the Manchester Statement today one is struck, even more forcibly than at first, by its seeming failure to address the reality of the situation which will be brought about by the promulgation of the new Canon. It has a potential for destruc-

tively damaging consequences if it is not treated with the
seriousness which it deserves, and with that charity for which it
is not unreasonable to look in the ambiguous circumstances in
which the Church of England has placed itself.

Because interest was drawn to the provisions made by the
Bishops for the pastoral care of those opposed to the ordination
of women to the priesthood, little immediate attention was given
to the arrangements which they proposed for discerning the
vocation of women deacons and women currently in training for
the diaconate.

"We are agreed that vocations should be tested at diocesan
level: the process would not involve attending a bishops' selection conference ....we shall be consulting in dioceses with
women deacons about the draft guidance and the arrangements
we shall each make...."[4]

The contrast, in every respect, with current well-established
procedures need not be underlined.

The number of women deacons who are not recommended
for advancement to the priesthood at this time will be an
interesting statistic, if it is ever published.

I am not sure that all women deacons will welcome this
special arrangement, even when they make allowance for the
unusual circumstances which prompted it. It is too reminiscent
of that brand of patronising unequal treatment against which so
many of them have protested for so long. There must have been
good reasons for suggesting this particular approach, but it will
not be surprising if the Bishops are deemed to have been less
solicitous of the finer sensibilities of some deacons than perhaps
either one would have expected or the situation required.

An unlooked for result of this proposal may be to cause
people to reflect more closely than for some time upon the
Church's selection procedures. Why should it not always be
conducted at diocesan level with the candidates involved in
setting up the process? Had this suggestion come as part of a
considered revision it might have been welcomed warmly. However this is to be a "one off" device for a particular purpose after

which, presumably, the old procedures will be resumed.

Having disposed speedily of the proposals for discerning vocations, the Bishops turned their attention to the "arrangements which will be necessary to ensure episcopal oversight and pastoral care for all the members of the Church of England following the coming into effect of the legislation."[5]

The problem confronting the Bishops, expressed in that way, lulled this reader, momentarily, into expecting proposals which took very serious account of the continuing divided response to the legislation, a response which the Bishops were at some pains to emphasise is wholly acceptable.[6] They would have to be seen also to have addressed the legal difficulties that would be encountered if they were serious in their wish to make, not only what they deemed to be adequate, but also what those they were addressing would find acceptable provision for alternative pastoral care. Sadly, as one read on, it became clear that there was to be a continuance of that policy of marginalisation towards the traditionalists which had been evident on other occasions.

Their thinking started from the ideas outlined at their meeting in June 1992.[7] However, they would have done better to start with the recognition of the consequences of the state of impaired communion which will be brought about by the ordination of women to the priesthood.

The Bishops had been addressed by *Forward in Faith* prior to their meeting. They were asked to provide an acceptable form of Alternative Episcopal Oversight, which took account of this. Despite the Bishops' expressed wish "to give every reassurance that we can",[8] in their response there appears to be an underlying reluctance to come to grips with the problem in its fullness and make such provisions as will be commensurate with the division which will have been brought about.

The Bishops' "encourage a willingness on the part of all to listen with respect to the views of those from whom they differ, and to afford a recognition of the value and integrity of each other's position within the Church."[9] One would hope still that part of that listening process will lead the Bishops to see that charity, as well as natural justice, requires that they go very much further than they have done so far in making adequate and acceptable provision for those who wish to remain within the tradition of the Apostolic Church in the Church of England. To have passed this particular piece of legislation with explicit reliance on its subsequent "reception" by the Church, means that a uniquely ambiguous situation has been brought about in which care has to be taken to provide sustaining sacramental structures which are acceptable to those who remain opposed. The difficulties inherent in the situation were stated clearly in the Second Report by the House of Bishops.

"We all recognise that there is a very particular problem when what is being tested in the reception process is not just a doctrine to be discussed but a doctrine that is embodied in persons, and more especially, embodied in the ordered ministry which effects an essential bond of communion of the Church. Where the Church's order is concerned, the process of reception may thus mean an impairing of communion while the open process of reception takes its course. Any impairing of communion is a painful process and it is the local church that is likely to experience it most acutely: what is tolerable between Provinces is increasingly difficult between dioceses or parishes within the same geographical area. This is particularly so in the parochial system of the Church of England. While we all recognise the difficulties in submitting the ordination of women to an open process of reception, the possibility remains of communion of faith, life and witness on the basis of carefully worked out safeguards."[10]

The process had to be embodied in Canon Law for it to get under way. Nevertheless, in a very real sense, the jury is still out and likely to remain so for some time, with no guarantee that it will return the expected verdict!

The Bishops' Report continues:

"Even if the reception process is completed by the Church of England, the decision still has to be accepted by the entire Anglican Communion and indeed by the Universal Church before it can be deemed to be the mind of Christ for his Church."[11]

In this uncertain but openly-anticipated situation, those opposed had looked for better safeguards than the Manchester Statement provides.

The confusion in which the Church of England is now moving is summed up in the following statement:

"differing views about the ordination of women to the priesthood can continue to be held with integrity within the Church of England."[12]

This will not bear close examination. The matter with which we are concerned is not a matter of opinion but the recognition of a person's sacramental identity and the ministry which proceeds from it. Quite properly, Canon Law does not allow for "differing views". Canon A4 states unequivocally:

"those who are so made, ordained or consecrated Bishops, priests or deacons, according to the said Ordinal, are lawfully made, ordained, or consecrated and ought to accounted both by themselves and others, to be truly Bishops, priests or deacons."

Once the Canon has been promulged there is no question but that those ordained thereafter will be ordained lawfully. Whether their ordination is also regular by any traditional understanding of Canon Law and Provincial authority is a matter which is open to serious doubt.

A former Bishop of Oxford examined some of the issues raised by the question of the ordination of women to the priesthood nearly fifty years ago. He said:

" . . . . it is a first principle that, where the integrity of the sacraments is in question, the Church must always take the safer course, and act on certainties and not on probabilities."[13]

That principle remains unchanged and with others of equal significance lies at the heart of the present dispute.

If, as the Bishops wish to maintain, "differing views . . . . can continue to be held with integrity within the Church of England"[14] how is Canon A4 to be interpreted? It alone will have the force of law. Once the new Canon is promulged, the

Manchester Statement, in this respect at least, must appear an empty form of words marking only a stage in the politics of a developing situation.

The Bishops addressed the matter of future appointments and said:

" .... we remain determined that the process of selection for ordination should remain fair, .... and should not discriminate between candidates on the ground of their views ... "

"There should not be any such discrimination in preferment of priests to the episcopate or other senior positions in the Church."[15]

These assurances are to be welcomed. They would have been welcomed even more warmly had the Bishops agreed to embody them in legislative form. Justice requires that there be the possibility of redress if there are proven instances of discrimination, either in the process of selection for ordination, or in the matter of preferment of priests to the Episcopate and other senior positions in the church. If there is no intention of exercising discrimination on the part of the Bishops and those involved in the various selection procedures, there should be no objection to providing a legal safeguard which will never have to be invoked.

But what are we to make now of earlier statements? In February 1987 the House of Bishops presented a report to the General Synod in which it was made quite clear that:

"Once a province has expressed its mind in favour of the ordination of women to the priesthood and proceeded to ordain women it would be anomalous to appoint a bishop who was actively opposed to the mind of the province and in particular opposed to the common mind of the college of Bishops."[16]

Earlier in the same Report it had been claimed that:

"It is difficult to see that a bishop who was unable to recognise the orders of a woman priest could minister as a diocesan Bishop in a diocese where there were already women priests."[17]

Later in the same document there is the bald statement that:

"These recommendations do not require legislation. Rather

they are ones which we hope will, as the case may be, be respected by the Crown Appointments Commission, or be dealt with in the Code of Practice."[18]

What reason is there to suppose that the Bishops have changed their mind in this matter in the intervening six years? Indeed, I would suspect that their attitude has hardened. The inevitable outcome of this policy cannot but be marginalisation leading eventually to elimination of the traditional catholic position within the Church of England. Sadly, with it will come, the equally inevitable departure from the Church of England of those for whom no longer any satisfactorily adequate sacramental provision can be made.

This is a situation about which some Bishops appear to be complacent. It cannot be matter of indifference to the members of the Parliamentary Ecclesiastical Committee whose brief is to consider the legislation and to report to Parliament as "to the expediency thereof, especially with relation to the constitutional rights of all Her Majesty's subjects."

In another part of the Statement the Bishops express their "firm intention to maintain the ecclesial integrity of the Church...while acknowledging the need to accommodate a diversity of convictions, particularly in matters relating to the Church's sacramental life."[19]

Even when allowance is made for the hasty composition of the document, this can be read only in a way which leads one to suppose that a significant number of the Bishops do not understand the reasons which compel those opposed to seek alternative episcopal oversight in the form for which it is asked.

It is one thing to live happily in a Church which accepts that its individual members may, from time to time, lay emphasis on particular aspects of the corporate faith, or on an aspect of the whole truth about a particular Sacrament, without detriment to that whole; it is altogether another matter to attempt to provide a focus of unity for diametrically-opposed views about the sacramental identity of some of the ministers of that Church in the person of a Bishop who, by ordaining women to the priesthood, has departed from Catholic tradition and thereby brought about impairment of communion within the Church.

Anglicans have had long experience of the former state of affairs and allusion is made to this in the Statement—

"We believe that the Anglican ethos and tradition which has been developed under God through our experience and history gives us particular resources for living through our present disagreements and uncertainties and doing so together."[20]

But the division introduced into the Church by the Bishops at that time will be altogether novel, and there is no helpful precedent for guidance from history for a situation which is most kindly described as one of doctrinal and sacramental pluralism within a contrived semblance of unity. (An earlier generation would have described it less euphemistically and much more harshly!)

Great emphasis is laid on the commitment to the maintenance of the "unity of each diocese under the jurisdiction of the diocesan bishop."[21].

Few would demur from the view that unity is fundamental to the Church's identity and mission, but it is difficult to share the view, which appears to be implied in the Statement, that jurisdiction by itself will make a substantial contribution towards sustaining that unity. Regretfully, attention has to be drawn, yet again, to the harsh reality of the situation which will exist in the Church of England when the Canon is promulged; to the difference between what will be *de jure* and what will be the *de facto* state of affairs brought about by that promulgation and the ordinations following from it.

One further consequence of the disunity that will characterise the life of the Church of England at that time relates to the difficulty which priests opposed to the Measure will have in swearing the oaths that are required at services of Institution and Induction with integrity after the Canon has been promulged. At a personal level it will present serious problems of conscience and at a pastoral level it could result in some priests staying in posts long after the time when, on their own admission, they should have moved.

It is to be regretted deeply that some Bishops were led to suppose that the validity of their sacramental ministry, subsequent to their ordaining a woman to the priesthood was being called in question.[22] No informed Anglican would have difficulty in endorsing the view expressed recently by the Bishop of Chichester who said:

"Such a view would be difficult to reconcile with the principles of sacramental validity evolved by St Augustine through the Donatist controversy, re-examined in the eleventh century controversy over simoniacal ordinations and formally stated by St Thomas Aquinas. There is an important distinction between invalidity and irregularity. A Bishop who ordains a woman has broken the historic canons of the Church and brought about a state of impaired communion. His action has been irregular and in consequence many people will consider that they can no longer accept his ministry, but I have not yet seen rigorously argued out the full consequences of such irregularity."[23]

Failure on the part of the Bishops to give careful attention to the position succinctly stated by Dr Kemp in his concluding sentence can lead only to a failure to understand why the Bishops' statement –

"We envisage that any bishop appointed to assist us in making any extended sacramental provision will remain in full communion with all members of the House of Bishops irrespective of whether or not such members have ordained women priests"[24]– does not command ready assent.

What understanding of Communion makes such a statement possible? Later the Bishops say: "There are many aspects of communion: it is not an all or nothing state of relationship."[25] One can only conclude that the difference between full communion and impaired communion is not the painful matter for some of the Bishops that it is for a large number of other members of the Church. All this savours too much of that fantastic Looking Glass world conjured up by Lewis Carroll. You may remember that in conversation with Alice, Humpty Dumpty said in rather a scornful tone:

"When *I* use a word it means just what I choose it to mean–

neither more nor less."

"The question is" said Alice "whether you *can* make words mean so many different things."

"The question is" said Humpty Dumpty "which is to be master–that's all."

Alice was much too puzzled to say anything...."[26]

Concluding, the Bishops outlined the practical measures they propose to deal with the situation. Apparently they are tentative and may entail:

"a diocesan bishop not himself ordaining women while permitting his suffragans or assistants to do so;

a diocesan bishop authorising a suffragan or assistant bishop from within the diocese to minister on his behalf to clergy and parishes whose views on this issue differ from his own;

a diocesan bishop, with the approval of the Primate of the Province concerned, making such arrangements with a bishop (whether diocesan, suffragan or assistant) from a neighbouring diocese."[27]

Canons C 18(4) and Canon C 20 determine the relation between a diocesan bishop and suffragan and assistant bishops in a diocese. They act under commission from him. It is the Church of England's understanding of the legal maxim *Quod facit alium facit per se.*

Some have seen in the distinction made between "permitting" in the first proposal and "authorising" in the second proposal the seed of an idea which might be explored further. A Bishop holding a commission not from the Diocesan, might be authorised to minister within a diocese, the diocesan acquiescing in that arrangement. Some would hope that, informed by a spirit of charity, an acceptable form of Alternative Episcopal Oversight could be developed on a regional basis along those lines.

The suggestion which attracted immediate publicity–the appointment of three Provincial Visitors–needs further development before it can be assessed properly.[28]

The Statement concludes with the promise that "in the coming months we intend to discuss with our clergy and people precisely what arrangements on these lines are necessary in each diocese and how they would operate."[29]

It says also that "at our meeting in June we will seek in the light of discussion in dioceses and in the Church at large to give more detailed guidance on the arrangements which will operate."[30]

Those who are opposed to the Measure should make clear, beyond all doubt, that they are anxious to take part in those discussions, either personally or by adequate representation. They are the people most immediately concerned, anxious to continue as members of the Church of England, albeit in a state of impaired communion which was none of their making.

If the Manchester Statement proves to be the last word in the matter from the House of Bishops the future for traditionalists is bleak. For whatever reasons, either the constraints of Canon Law or an unwillingness to go beyond what the Statement offers, the Bishops must be deemed to have failed to provide the long-promised safeguards. It makes adequate provision for those whose opposition is grounded solely in prejudice or anti-feminist principle. For others, not coming from that starting point, deeply conscious of the valued ministry which women offer to the life of the Church already, but even more conscious of the requirements of catholic order in a church which claims to be part of the Apostolic Church, there is little in the document which addresses their need realistically.

Some will feel that the Church of England has changed its identity and that in consequence it is no longer their spiritual home. Others, mainly priests with family commitments, or who are not of an age to benefit from the fullest financial arrangements, will be forced to stay with compromised consciences. Others will stay in a state of pained confusion and uneasy conscience uncertain yet about what God requires of them.

As one of the latter I have been searching for practical advice and a theological perspective. The first I have found in some words from Sir Thomas More's *Utopia*.

"What part soever you have taken upon you, playe that aswel

as you can and make the best of it: and doe not therefore disturbe and brynge out of order the whole matter, bycause that an other, which is meryer and better commeth to your remembraunce . . . . you must not forsake the shippe in a tempeste, because you cannot rule and kepe downe the wyndes . . . . But you must with a crafty wile and subtell trayne studye and endevoure youre selfe, asmuche as in you lyeth, to handle the matter wyttelye and handsomelye for the purpose, and that whyche you can not turne to good, so order it that it be not very badde."[31] An eloquent exhortation to an unattractive prospect.

With that must go the theological perspective found in the words of a Mirfield Father[32].

" . . . . much of the meaning of all this lies hidden in Gethsemane. Blind, cruel, pointless, total blackness, an agony beyond words . . . . Agony which has been accepted, not passively, but has been faced and lived through. And from which sprang incredible victory and joy. And when the night goes on or the darkness comes and goes, when faith and hope lies shattered, there comes the faint knowledge that God knows what it costs, that he has been along the path and he still walks with us."

**Notes**

1 Statement of the House of Bishops. 14 January 1993. (Referred to hereafter as Manchester.)
2 *The Tablet* 27.2.93 p.268
3 GS 764:44 *The Ordination of Women to the Priesthood. A Report by the House of Bishops.* General Synod 1987
4 Manchester para 1(a)
5 Ibid para 1(b)
6 Ibid para 4
7 Ibid para 9
8 Ibid para 3
9 Ibid para 4
10 GS 829:175 *The Ordination of Women to the Priesthood. A Second Report by the House of Bishops of the General Synod of the Church of England.* General Synod 1988
11 Ibid para 177
12 Manchester para 4

13 Kirk, K.E., *Beauty and Bands.* London 1955 p.188
14 Manchester para 4
15 Ibid para 7
16 GS 764:40
17 Ibid para 38
18 Ibid para 51
19 Manchester para 8
20 Ibid para 5
21 Ibid para 8
22 Ibid para 11
23 Address to the Federation of Catholic Priests: Chichester
24 Manchester para 11
25 Ibid para 6
26 Carroll, Lewis, *Through the Looking Glass and What Alice Found There.* 1872
27 Manchester para 12
28 Ibid para 13
29 Ibid para 14
30 Ibid para 15
31 More, Thomas, *Utopia.* London (Everyman Library) 1910
32 Beasley, H., *The Best Is Yet To Be.* Mirfield Publications ed.

# XII

# Implications for the Church.

## Edward Knapp–Fisher

Few would disagree with Thomas Campbell's observation that 'coming events cast their shadows before'. The present turmoil in the Church of England was foreshadowed by the action of the Episcopal Church in the United States of America when it became the first province in the Anglican Communion to ordain women to the priesthood. Since then a number of other provinces have followed suit: but the implications of these ordinations were perhaps not fully realized or frankly faced until the General Synod decided to make legal provision for them to take place in England. Among other consequences of this decision is the likelihood that provinces elsewhere which have hitherto hesitated to take this step will now follow the example of the Mother Church. It is certain that when the Archbishop of Canterbury, the senior Primate of the Anglican Communion, himself ordains women this will be widely regarded as an official endorsement of a practice which will be generally viewed as normal throughout the Communion.

It is the conviction of many Anglicans that the decision to ordain women runs counter to the historical claim of the Church of England to be the authentic expression of the Catholic Church in this country.This claim is clearly articulated in the form of the *Declaration of Assent* by which all who are ordained, licensed, instituted or installed are required to affirm that 'the Church of England is part of the One, Holy, Catholic and Apostolic Church'. In respect of the ordained ministry, the Catholic tradition is plainly affirmed in the *Preface to the Ordinal*:

> It is evident unto all men diligently reading Holy Scripture and ancient Authors, that from the Apostles' time there have been these Orders of Ministers in Christ's Church: Bishops, Priests and Deacons... And therefore, these Orders (are to) be continued, and reverently used, and esteemed, in the Church of England.

It is equally apparent that for nineteen hundred years the unbroken tradition of the universal Church was that only men could be ordained to ministerial priesthood. The ordination of women to the priesthood has no warrant in Scripture or Tradition. Dr Eric Kemp, Bishop of Chichester, spoke for many when he stated, after the General Synod vote, that 'the decision will raise for a number of people the question whether they can regard the Church of England as any longer a true part of the One, Holy, Catholic and Apostolic Church'.

The scale of the opposition within the Church of England seems to have taken the supporters of women's ordination by surprise; and it is tragic that the process of Anglican disintegration is moving towards its climax during the Decade of Evangelism. This is a period when differences between us should be left, at least temporarily, in abeyance; all other activities subordinated to praying and working for Christian unity. Ecclesiastical organization and common sense combine to demonstrate that unity and mission are inextricably bound up with one another. Our claim to proclaim the gospel of reconciliation will carry little conviction while our divisions not only remain but continue to increase. The cynical, sceptical and divided world is justified in bidding us first set our own house in order before we expect others to listen to what we have to say.

The issue of women's ordination, which has increased our

domestic disunity, has also widened the gap between ourselves and the Roman Catholic and Eastern Orthodox Churches. Considerable progress in negotiations between us has been largely nullified. Over the past thirty years remarkable advances had been made in relations between Rome and Canterbury. But western and eastern Catholicism alike have described the action of Anglican provinces in ordaining women as a serious new obstacle to closer unity. The situation has been accurately assessed in a leading Roman Catholic journal.

> At the level of Roman Catholic–Anglican inter-Church dialogue, there is going to be a sea-change, whatever solution is reached within the Church of England itself. ARCIC, which over twenty years has made progress that might have seemed inconceivable, has been based on Rome's acknowledgement of the Church of England as– to use Paul VI's term–a 'sister Church'. It was understood that this particular dialogue took place on privileged terrain. That understanding will cease. The Church of England's decision to ordain women to the priesthood seems to rule out the mutual recognition of ministries and shared communion which had appeared a real prospect. (*The Tablet.* 16.1.93. 'Difficult days for Christian Unity'.)

The crux of the matter, however, is not the ordination of women but the major question of the nature and *locus* of *Authority in the Church*. Preoccupation with the particular issue at the expense of tackling the problem of authority is to deal with the symptoms instead of the roots of our present malaise. The encyclical *Humanae Vitae* has been described as one of the most disastrous 'Church-renders'. The issue of birth (or conception) control with which it was specifically concerned was of secondary importance to the problem of authority in the church. The manner in which the encyclical was prepared and presented raised the whole question of the authority of the Pope. The debate about the ordination of women to the priesthood in the Church of England, which led up to the vote of the

General Synod on 11 November 1992, similarly raised the issue of authority, in this case that of Synods in England and throughout the Anglican Communion.

Synodical government poses no problems for Christians committed to the doctrine of the parity of ministries, who organize their communities on democratic lines; but for hierarchically ordered Churches where authority is vested in bishops there can be no logical place for synods invested with *legislative* powers. It is true that in the General Synod, as in the synods of other Anglican provinces, constitutional provision is made for voting by houses. But there are many who wish to abolish a practice which is neither wholly satisfactory nor necessarily permanent. 'It has become increasingly clear that the Church of England has not yet effectively resolved the inherent tension between a synodical and episcopal form of government.' (Adrian Hastings: *Robert Runcie*. p.69.) This tension can surely be resolved only if in episcopal Churches synods are constituted as consultative and advisory (*not* legislative) bodies, which provide the bishops with the advice and expertise necessary to enable them to make informed decisions.

Press accounts of the General Synod debate suggest that while allusions were made to *authority* the subject did not receive a great deal of serious discussion. Although some attention was given to such matters as *development in doctrine* and the Biblical interpretation of *headship*, it is difficult to know to what extent members were influenced by *theological* considerations. What seems clear is that in the preliminary propaganda and the final debate proponents of both points of view appeared to rely largely on psychological, sociological and pragmatic arguments. In this respect the Archbishop of Canterbury surely spoke for and appealed to the great majority of Anglicans in the pews: 'We are in danger of not being heard if women are exercising leadership in every area of our society's life save the ordained priesthood'. The Bishop of Southwark argued his case on similar grounds: 'I cannot with any integrity challenge the injustice of society and turn a blind eye to the apparent injustice in the Church which prevents women from testing their vocation to the priesthood'. Such arguments make a powerful appeal, not least to the many who demonstrate their ignorance of the real matter at issue by remarking that if the Free Churches have women *ministers* there can be no reason why the Church of England should not have women *priests*. Statements like this provide some justification for the harsh judgement of a Roman Catholic commentator that 'so long as the Church of England is an outgrowth of the national culture . . . it cannot risk distancing itself too far from the standards and values that the nation believes in'. A tendency to conform to the spirit and *mores* of the age is not, however, confined to national Churches.

It is hard to believe that decisions based on such arguments will necessarily lead to actions in conformity with the will of God. Credibility is still further stretched by the recognition by the Lambeth Conference of 1988 of provincial autonomy in the Anglican Communion, with its corollary, the vague notion of 'impaired communion'. None would dispute that there must be development in doctrine as well as in the forms and formulae through which it has to be articulated and communicated. 'Here below, to live is to change, and to be perfect is to have changed often.' (J.H. Newman) The problem of discerning the guidance of the Holy Spirit, of distinguishing between true and false developments, is exacerbated when Christians are divided. There must, however, surely be a stronger probability of His speaking through the long and unbroken tradition of Western Catholicism and Eastern Orthodoxy than through a single synod of one part of that fragment of the Church Universal which is the Anglican Communion. The ability of the majority of any elected body to decide on matters of which they may know little, is at least open to doubt.

In the General Synod debate the Bishop of London spoke for many when he said that while he was committed to the full-time ministry of women, he was *not yet* convinced that they should be priests. Those of us who share this point of view are not prepared to say that it is intrinsically impossible for a woman to be a priest. We believe that there are some cogent theological objections to it; but whether or not these can be regarded as decisive can be judged only by the Universal Church, far more united in faith and love than at present it is.

We have looked at some of the implications of the General Synod vote for the Anglican Communion, whose disintegration it threatens, and for the universal Church, to whose quest for unity it has created new obstacles. What, finally, are the implications for individual Anglicans of differing shades of churchmanship who question both what the Synod has decided and its authority for so doing?

Their options are to remain Anglicans if in conscience they can do so, or to seek another home.

The Manchester meeting of the English bishops in January produced proposals designed to enable 'traditionalists' to remain with integrity within the Church of England. A key proposal provides for the appointment of three itinerant episcopal Provincial Visitors. Further details are promised later. Here again the impression is given that principle is being sacrificed to a pragmatic attempt to maintain the appearance of Anglican solidarity at any price. *Episcopi vagantes* have long been regarded as theological anomalies; and it is not easy to reconcile this, or any other scheme for alternative episcopal oversight, with episcopacy as it has been traditionally received and understood. A bishop is a symbol of the unity and catholicity of the Church. He acts not alone but in collegial association with his brother bishops with whom he is fully in communion. In this context 'impaired communion' seems to be a euphemism for a theological absurdity. (But this matter is considered in another essay.) In fact it looks as if such a scheme, if adopted, might well produce just such a 'church within a church' as the bishops are reported to have been reluctant to contemplate.

The only other available option is to seek another home. But where are those who conclude that they must part company with Canterbury to go? Evangelicals may have a number of alternatives. Catholics, unless they form or join a sect, could choose only between Rome and Constantinople. With Eastern Orthodoxy they would have doctrinal affinity, but might find it hard to feel at home in a liturgical and cultural ethos very different from anything to which they had been accustomed. With Roman Catholicism a minority of Anglican Catholics might feel immediately at home; but many more, although finding the liturgy and general ethos familiar and congenial, would have problems about points of doctrine, notably those relating to the Pope and the Blessed Virgin Mary. A major additional problem for *ordained* Anglicans is the unpalatable fact that the validity of their Orders is still denied by Rome. They cannot abandon their conviction, confirmed by experience, that the sacraments they administered were means of grace and that their pastoral ministry has been abundantly blessed. They could not deny their past.

Roman Catholicism, too, is in a state of transition and is confronted by problems of *authority*. Indeed unresolved problems relating to the nature and exercise of authority in the Church underlie many of the other relatively minor differences which still divide Christians. Many of us believe that these issues can be resolved only if the complementarity of conciliarity and primacy, recommended by the Anglican/Roman Catholic International Commission, is generally endorsed and put into practice. 'Anglicans sometimes fear the prospect of over-centralization, Roman Catholics the prospect of doctrinal incoherence. Faith, banishing fear, might see simply the prospect of the right balance between a primacy serving the unity and a conciliarity maintaining the just diversity of the *koinonia* of all the Churches.'

To stay where we are or to go elsewhere? That is our dilemma and it presents us with no easy option. Any precipitate and ill-considered action is unlikely to lead to God's will being done. Many factors have to be taken into account—our personal relationships and circumstances and the effects of any action we may take on those who love and trust us. Conflicting considerations have to be carefully and prayerfully weighed. Whatever we decide, one thing is certain: we shall never escape the anomalies, inadequacies and defects which are inseparable from each and every part of the Church Militant here on earth.

> Most gracious God, we humbly beseech Thee for Thy
> Holy Catholic Church:
> Fill it with Thy truth; in all truth with all peace.
> Where it is corrupt, purge it;
> Where it is in error, direct it;
> Where anything is amiss, reform it;
> Where it is right, strengthen and confirm it;
> Where it is in want, furnish it;
> Where it is divided and rent asunder, make up the
> breaches of it;
> Through Jesus Christ our Lord.

# Appendix 1

# The Significance of the Coronation Oath in the Present Crisis

## David Samuel

The Monarch has solemnly promised and undertaken, in the Coronation Oath, "to the utmost of [her] power" to "maintain and preserve inviolably the settlement of the Church of England, and the doctrine, worship, discipline, and government thereof, as by law established in England". In the present crisis precipitated by the proposal to ordain females to the priesthood of the Church of England, it is important that the full nature of the Coronation Oath and its implications be examined and understood.

First, the undertaking by the sovereign is a most solemn one. It is no mere formality or empty ritual. It is a real and sacred duty binding upon the Crown to maintain and preserve the integrity of the Church of England. "To maintain" means to carry on, to keep up unimpaired. "To preserve" is to keep safe from harm and injury. The meaning of the two words is in some respects similar, but it is clear that their purpose is to supplement and reinforce each other and to emphasise the importance of the commitment undertaken. They are qualified by the adverb "inviolably" which means "without break, injury or infraction". The cumulative effect of the clause is significant. It means that the oath engages the sovereign solemnly to keep safe, unimpaired, without break, loss or injury the integrity of the Church of England, in its doctrine, worship, discipline and government, as established by law.

The doctrine of the Church of England is defined in Canon A5, which states, in the historic Anglican way, that it is "grounded in the Holy Scriptures and in such teachings of the ancient Fathers and Councils of the Church as are agreeable to the said Scriptures. In particular such doctrine is to be found in the Thirty-Nine Articles of Religion, the Book of Common Prayer, and the Ordinal". It is clear from this account of the doctrine of the Church of England that the purpose of the Coronation Oath and the precise terms in which it is couched is to maintain and preserve in the manner we have defined the Catholic and Apostolic nature of the Church of England. This is supported by the wording of the Ordinal which lays special emphasis upon such Catholic and Apostolic doctrine and order. Those to be ordained to the Priesthood must promise "always to minister the Doctrine and Sacraments, and the Discipline of Christ, as the Lord hath commanded, *and as this Church and Realm hath received the same*, according to the commandments of God". The stress is upon continuity and identity in order that nothing might be done to impair or injure the character of the Church of England and its claim to be part of the one Holy, Catholic and Apostolic Church. To maintain this character is the solemn and fundamental duty of the sovereign as the Supreme Governor of the Church of England. Whatever changes may have taken place in the nature of the monarchy in this country over the last four hundred years none can be deemed to have deprived the sovereign of the power to fulfil this duty and to carry out the terms of her solemn commitment to the Church.

The making of female priests, as is proposed in the Measure passed in General Synod in November last, is a clear breach and infraction of the Catholic doctrine and order of the Church of England. No woman candidate for the priesthood can promise "to minister the Doctrine and Sacraments, and the Discipline of Christ, as the Lord hath commanded, and as this Church and Realm hath received the same..." for women have never before been admitted to the priesthood. The General Synod has no power to change the Catholic and Apostolic character of the Church for, as is so clearly stated in the Worship and Doctrine

Measure sections 4(1) and 4(3), it has no power to change the doctrine of the Church of England. It certainly has no power to alter or **supersede** the Services of the Book of Common Prayer, and such alternative services as it authorises it does so for a term of years after which they must be renewed or lapse. The Priests (Ordination of Women) Measure, however, proposes a radical change which will permanently impair the Catholic credentials of the National Church. It is the clear duty of the Crown to prevent this happening and "to maintain and preserve inviolably the settlement of the Church of England."

The manner in which the Crown is to do this must be consonant with the nature of constitutional monarchy. The sovereign cannot act unilaterally, but must act in and through parliament on the advice of her ministers. The doctrine of the Crown-in-Parliament requires parliament to act with and in the name of the sovereign to fulfil the purposes to which the Crown is committed. It is therefore every bit as much the duty of Parliament as of the Crown to see that the solemn undertaking of the Coronation Oath to maintain and preserve the National Church is carried out. If the Ecclesiastical Committee of Parliament entertains the least suspicion from the evidence before it that the Priests (Ordination of Women) Measure is an infraction of the Catholic and Apostolic character of the Church of England "as this Church and Realm hath received it" then it has in the name of the Crown a sacred duty to deem the Measure 'not expedient' and to return it to the General Synod.

If it is objected that the position taken in this paper excludes all change whatever in the practice of the Church of England and that that position is both unacceptable and untenable, it must be pointed out that the exclusion of all change is not aimed at in the Coronation Oath, but only such changes as may affect the constitution and standing of the Church of England as the Catholic Church of this nation. It is precisely these sorts of changes which the Priests (Ordination of Women) Measure would bring about.

# Appendix 2

**The Coronation Oath of Her Majesty Queen Elizabeth II Tuesday 2nd June 1953**

*Archbishop*: Will you to the utmost of your power maintain the laws of God and the true profession of the Gospel? Will you to the utmost of your power maintain in the United Kingdom the Protestant Reformed Religion established by law? Will you maintain and preserve inviolably the Settlement of the Church of England, and the doctrine, worship, discipline, and government thereof, as by law established in England? And will you preserve unto the Bishops and clergy, and to the Churches there committed to their charge, all such rights and privileges, as by law do or shall appertain to them or any of them?

*Queen*: All this I promise to do

# Appendix 3

**Correspondence between the Archbishop of Canterbury and Pope John Paul II, August–December 1988**

From: Lambeth Palace London SE1 7JU
6th August 1988

The Transfiguration of Our Lord
To: His Holiness Pope John Paul II

Your Holiness,

At the close of the twelfth Lambeth Conference of the Bishops of the Anglican Communion, I write to you to thank you for the presence of the Catholic Observers, for your personal letter assuring the Conference of your prayers, and to inform you directly of the results of our deliberations.

One of the happy features of our Conference has been the presence of Observers and Speakers from many churches. Among the speakers it was a particular pleasure to welcome Father Pierre Duprey, Secretary of the Vatican Secretariat for Promoting Christian Unity, who delivered an important response to my own opening address. Father Duprey carried your letter to the Conference and I read it to the plenary assembly of Bishops. The tactful courtesy in the manner of your reference to the known obstacle of the ordination of women was deeply appreciated.

Although the ordination of women to the priesthood and episcopate has been in the forefront of our deliberations, the principal issue before the Conference has actually been the underlying question of authority, the developing tradition of the

Church, and ecclesiology. I spoke at some length to the Conference of this, including the structures required for unity: the episcopate, conciliarity and primacy. I spoke specifically of the primacy you demonstrated in Assisi in 1986 in convoking the Day of Prayer for Peace. Of your office as Bishop of Rome I asked:

> "could not all Christians come to reconsider the kind of primacy exercised within the Early Church, a 'presiding in love' for the sake of the unity of the Churches"?

But the ecumenical pilgrimage has not yet reached this stage. In the meantime urgent questions have to be faced, new problems addressed and the mission of the Church exercised even in our separation. Thus in a number of Provinces of the Anglican Communion the question of the ordination of women to the priesthood, and now episcopate, arises. The Lambeth Conference has no juridical authority over the Anglican Communion. Nor do I. All the Provinces have the canonical authority to implement the mission of the Church as they deem right in their own culture. So the matter of the ordination of women, especially to the episcopate, has been deeply divisive.

Nevertheless, the overall ethos of the Lambeth Conference has been one of unity and communion despite deeply held differences. It is probable that some provinces, especially in North America, may shortly elect and consecrate a woman bishop. The Lambeth Conference resolved to respect this decision even if not all other bishops and provinces can yet recognize such a woman bishop. There will be the pain of some impairment of communion. Difficult as this is, it is, in the judgement of this conference, a more acceptable solution than a schism within the Anglican Communion. We are now urgently to examine the relations between Provinces which differ in practice on this matter. We recognize the ecumenical implications of this debate but know that the Catholic Church would also see a split in the Anglican Communion as a grave ecumenical obstacle.

I acknowledge that there is need for much more study of the

question of women's ordination. I also feel that this study should be conducted on an ecumenical basis. I was glad that this view was re-echoed in the response made to my opening address by Metropolitan John of Pergamos who is Co-Chairman of the Anglican/Orthodox dialogue and, of course, a member of the Catholic/Orthodox International Commission. He called for an exhaustive theological debate on this matter and said:

> "It seems to me that we have not even begun to treat the issue of the ordination of women as a theological problem at an ecumenical level."

It is my prayer that such ecumenical debate, involving all Christians, may be taken up and carried out in an atmosphere of trust and mutual respect.

The Conference went on to consider the responses of 23 autonomous Provinces to the Final Report of the Anglican/Roman Catholic International Commission. One of the most important tasks of the conference was to pronounce the consensus of the Anglican Communion on the Agreed Statements of the dialogue established by our predecessors in 1966. The Bishops, by a very large majority, recognized the ARCIC Agreed Statements on the eucharist and the ordained ministry as "consonant in substance with the faith of Anglicans". On authority the Agreed Statements were welcomed as "a firm basis" for the future dialogue. The complete text of these very positive Resolutions is in the hands of the Catholic Observers. They represent a very strong affirmation by the Anglican Communion about the results of our dialogue.

While the Bishops of the Anglican Communion realize that there will be no easy solution to the difficult question of the ordination of women, I see this strong affirmation of the work of ARCIC-I as a significant Anglican step towards "the mutual recognition of the ministries of our two Communions" of which we spoke in Canterbury together in May 1982.

In spite of obstacles the Bishops of the Anglican Communion are determined to continue to seek the unity Our Lord wills and to pursue the quest for the full visible unity to which our two Communions are committed.

May God bestow upon us this gift and the grace to receive it.

Your Holiness' Brother in Christ,

Robert Cantuar

**To The Most Reverend Robert Runcie Archbishop of Canterbury**
From the Vatican, 8th December 1988

I acknowledge with gratitude the letter which you sent to me at the close of the twelfth Lambeth Conference last August. Your thoughtfulness in informing me about the proceedings of the Conference is much appreciated. I see in this gracious gesture a further indication of the trust that exists between us and of the strong bond of communion by which we are already united.

In responding to your communication, I would first of all acknowledge the signs of openness to fuller communion with the Catholic Church which were evident at several points in the Conference, not least in your opening address and in the resolutions on the Final Report of ARCIC-1. At the same time, I must express my concern in respect of those developments at Lambeth which seem to have placed new obstacles in the way of reconciliation between Catholics and Anglicans. The Lambeth Conference's treatment of the question of women's ordination has created a new and perplexing situation for the members of the Second Anglican/Roman Catholic International Commission to whom, in 1982, we gave the mandate of studying "all that hinders the mutual recognition of the ministries of our Communions". The ordination of women to the priesthood in some provinces of the Anglican Communion, together with the recognition of the right of individual provinces to proceed with the ordination of women to the episcopacy, appears to pre-empt this study and effectively block the path to the mutual recognition of ministries.

The Catholic Church, like the Orthodox Church and the

Ancient Oriental Churches, is firmly opposed to this development, viewing it as a break with Tradition of a kind we have no competence to authorize. It would seem that the discussion of women's ordination in the Anglican Communion has not taken sufficiently into account the ecumenical and ecclesiological dimensions of the question. Since the Anglican Communion is in dialogue with the Catholic Church–as it is with the Orthodox Church and the Ancient Oriental Churches–it is urgent that this aspect be given much greater attention in order to prevent a serious erosion of the degree of communion between us.

I am aware that no final decision on the controversial question of women's ordination has been taken as far as the Church of England is concerned. I likewise understand the delicate nature of your own position, given the autonomy of each of the provinces that make up the Anglican Communion, as well as your anxiety over a possible split within that Communion. Since, however, as Archbishop of Canterbury you also represent the Anglican Communion in its relations with the Catholic Church, a highly problematic situation could certainly arise for those provinces opposed to women's ordination if there were women priests in the Church of England. In addressing Your Grace so directly on this matter, I would stress that my motivation is simply to serve the quest for unity to which our predecessors Pope Paul VI and Archbishop Michael Ramsey committed themselves in 1966; a commitment which you and I renewed during my visit to Canterbury in 1982.

Assuring you of my prayers as we persevere in the search for that unity willed by the Lord for all his disciples, I renew my warm fraternal greetings in our Saviour Jesus Christ, the Eternal High Priest.

Joannes Paulus PPII

# Appendix 4

Anglican-Orthodox Joint Doctrinal Commission,
Athens July 1978

# The Orthodox position on the Ordination of Women to the Priesthood

The Orthodox members of the Commission unanimously affirm the following:

(1) God created mankind in his image as male and female, establishing a diversity of functions and gifts. These functions are complementary but, as St Paul insists (1 Cor. 12), not all are interchangeable. In the life of the Church, as in that of the family, God has assigned certain tasks and forms of ministry specifically to the man, and others–different, yet no less important–to the woman. There is every reason for Christians to oppose current trends which make men and women interchangeable in their functions and roles, and thus lead to the dehumanization of life.

(2) The Orthodox Church honours a woman, the Holy Virgin Mary, the Theotokos, as the human person closest to God. In the Orthodox tradition women saints are given such titles as *megalomartys* (great martyr) and *isapostolos* (equal to the apostles). Thus it is clear that in no sense does the Orthodox Church consider women to be intrinsically inferior in God's eyes. Men and women are equal but different, and we need to

recognize this diversity of gifts. Both in discussion among themselves and in dialogue with other Christians the Orthodox recognize the duty of the Church to give women more opportunities to use their specific *charismata* (gifts) for the benefit of the whole people of God. Among the ministries (*diakoniai*) exercised by women in the Church we note the following:

(i) ministries of a diaconal and philanthropic kind, involving the pastoral care of the sick and needy, of refugees and many others, and issuing in various forms of social responsibility,

(ii) ministries of prayer and intercession, of spiritual help and guidance, particularly but not exclusively in connection with the monastic communities,

(iii) ministries connected with teaching and instruction, particularly in the field of the Church's missionary activity,

(iv) ministries connected with the administration of the Church.

This list is not meant to be exhaustive. It indicates some of the areas where we believe that women and men are called to work together in the service of God's Kingdom, and where the many *charismata* of the Holy Spirit may function freely and fruitfully in the building up of the Church and society.

(3) But, while women exercise this diversity of ministries, it is not possible for them to be admitted to the priesthood. The ordination of women to the priesthood is an innovation, lacking any basis whatever in Holy Tradition. The Orthodox Church takes very seriously the admonition of St Paul, where the Apostle states with emphasis, repeating himself twice: 'But if we or an angel from heaven, preaches to you anything else than what we have preached to you, let him be anathema. As we have already said, so I say to you now once more: if anyone preaches to you anything else than what you have received, let him be anathema' (Gal. 1.8-9).

From the time of Christ and the apostles onwards, the Church has ordained only men to the priesthood. Christians today are bound to remain faithful to the example of our Lord, to the testimony of Scripture, and to the constant and unvarying practice of the Church for two thousand years. In this constant and unvarying practice we see revealed the will of God and the testimony of the Holy Spirit, and we know that the Holy Spirit does not contradict himself.

(4) Holy Tradition is not static, but living and creative. Tradition is received by each succeeding generation in the same way, but in its own situation, and thus it is verified and enriched by the renewed experience that the People of God are continually gaining. On the basis of this renewed experience, the Spirit teaches us to be always responsive to the needs of the contemporary world. The Spirit does not bring us a new revelation, but enables us to relive the truth revealed once for all in Jesus Christ, and continuously present in the Church. It is important, therefore, to distinguish between innovations and the creative continuity of Tradition. We Orthodox see the ordination of women, not as part of this creative continuity, but as a violation of the apostolic faith and order of the Church.

(5) The action of ordaining women to the priesthood involves not simply a canonical point of Church discipline, but the basis of the Christian faith as expressed in the Church's ministries. If the Anglicans continue to ordain women to the priesthood, this will have a decisively negative effect on the issue of the recognition of Anglican Orders. Those Orthodox Churches which have partially or provisionally recognized Anglican Orders did so on the ground that the Anglican Church has preserved the apostolic succession; and the apostolic succession is not merely continuity in the outward laying on of hands, but signifies continuity in apostolic faith and spiritual life. By ordaining women, Anglicans would sever themselves from this continuity, and so any existing acts of recognition by the Orthodox would have to be reconsidered.

## Anglican Positions on the Ordination of Women to the Priesthood

(1) The Anglican members of the Commission are unanimous in their desire to accept and maintain the tradition of the gospel, to which the prophets and apostles bear witness, and to be true to it in the life of the Church. They are divided over the ways in which that tradition should respond to the pressures of the world, over the extent to which the tradition may develop and change, and over the criteria by which to determine what developments within it are legitimate and appropriate. In the case of the ordination of women differences have become particularly acute and divisive within the Anglican Communion, now that the convictions of those in favour of it have been translated into action in certain national churches.

(2) On this question there is a diversity of views in the Anglican Communion and among the members of the Commission. There are those who believe that the ordination of women to the priesthood and the episcopate is in no way consonant with a true understanding of the Church's catholicity and apostolocity, but rather constitutes a grave deformation of the Church's traditional faith and order. They therefore hope that under the guidance of the Holy Spirit, this practice will come to cease in our churches.

There are others who believe that the actions already taken constitute a proper extension and development of the Church's traditional ministry, and a necessary and prophetic response to the changing circumstances in which some churches are placed. They hope that in due time, under the guidance of the Spirit, these actions will be universally accepted.

There are others who regret the way in which the present action has been taken and believe that the time was not opportune nor the method appropriate for such action, although they see no absolute objection to it. Some of them hope that a way forward may be found which will allow for the distinct and complementary contributions of men and women to the Church's ordained ministry.

The minutes of the 1978 Athens Conference add the following presentation of Anglican views which were expressed at the time:

(1) Those Anglicans who in principle oppose the ordination of women do so for the reasons advanced by the Orthodox in this report. They would express their reasons as follows: the claim of the Anglican Communion to be catholic means that compelling reasons must be demonstrated for the rightness of such a break with catholic tradition. Those who oppose such a break believe that such reasons have not been forthcoming. On the contrary, they believe that there are fundamental reasons why such a break should not be made. These, in their judgement, come from a consideration of the Person of Christ. Although there is neither maleness nor femaleness in God, it was in a male that the word was made flesh and humanity in all its fullness was united to the Godhead. They believe that this fact expresses the truth that the initiative in our redemption lies wholly with God, to whom the response of humanity must be creative obedience. For a woman to be the icon or sacramental expression of Christ as Head of the Church seems to them to be in opposition to the biblical images of the Church in relation to God, which consistently stress that humanity and the Church must be feminine in relation to God.

The New Testament indicates that the issue of headship and authority, however qualified, cannot be divorced either from the created relationship between man and woman, for instance in marriage, or from the instituted relationship between the ordained ministry and the congregation. They believe that a male priest must be the symbol and image of Christ as

Bridegroom, whereas women, supremely exemplified in Mary, to whom was given the highest vocation of any created being, must be the symbol and image of the response of humanity in creative obedience. They believe that the God-given nature of the ministerial priesthood includes the fact that it is male. A refusal to accept this fact leads in their judgement, not only to a distortion of man's understanding of his relationship to God, but also to a distortion of his understanding of the redemption of the deepest aspects of his humanity. Finally, the opponents believe that the ordination of women to the priesthood is divisive because it is wrong, rather than wrong because it is divisive.

(2) Those members of the Commission who advocate the ordination of women to the priesthood now do so because they believe that the Church's tradition must grow and develop if the Church is to remain faithful to its mission to the world. More particularly, they believe that this is a true development, under the guidance of the Holy Spirit, of the patterns of ministry to which God has been calling some Churches in response to major changes in the ordering of society. The vocations of women who offer themselves for the priestly ministry require therefore to be tested, and none of the arguments, either from Scripture or tradition, advanced against such vocations seem to those who hold this position to be in principle convincing. In particular they hold that arguments which suggest that priests must be male in order either to represent the maleness of God, a position held by no one in this Commission, or because the maleness of Christ is of soteriological significance, are based on serious doctrinal errors. Since priesthood represents humanity to God and God to humanity, it is humanity and not maleness which is the decisive qualification for exercising priesthood, just as in Christ, according to catholic doctrine, it is his humanity which is of soteriological significance and not the accidents of his humanity. Further they argue that to insist on an all-male priesthood in societies which have abandoned all-male leadership in other areas of life is in effect to distort the meaning of

Christian priesthood. This may lead to serious distortions in doctrine. Thirdly, they believe that the ordination of women would lead to an enrichment of the Christian priesthood by bringing to it women's gifts and wisdom, as well as by deepening the Christian understanding of the divine saving initiative in Jesus Christ which is represented by the priesthood.

(3) There are other members of the Commission who, while they find these theological arguments valid and convincing, yet believe for reasons of an ecclesiological nature that action in this matter should not be taken precipitately.

# Appendix 5

# House Of Bishops

*Statement by the House following its meeting in Manchester,
11-14 January 1993*

1. At our meeting in Manchester we have reflected together with all our episcopal colleagues on the new situation facing the Church of England following the decision of the General Synod to give final approval to the draft legislation on the ordination of women to the priesthood. In particular we have considered:

> a) what process should be followed (assuming that Parliament approves the legislation) to discern the vocation to the priesthood of women deacons and women currently in training for the diaconate. We are agreed that vocations should be tested at diocesan level: the process would not involve attending a bishops' selection conference. But in order to ensure broad parity between dioceses in the arrangements they make, we have discussed draft guidance to dioceses on the process, which is being revised in the light of our discussions. We shall be consulting in dioceses with women deacons about the draft guidance and the arrangements we shall each make, and will confirm the final text of the guidance when we meet again in June;
>
> b) what arrangements will be necessary to ensure continued episcopal oversight and pastoral care for all members of the Church of England following the coming into effect of the legislation. In the remainder of this statement we have focused on this latter question.

2. The majority of bishops, like the majority of those who voted throughout the synodical structure, welcome the Synod's decision and look forward to new gifts which the ministry of women priests will bring to the life of the Church.

3. Others in the Church, however, remain opposed to the ordination of women to the priesthood and it is to them in particular that we have been giving our attention at this time, in order to give every reassurance that we can. Our discussions have been guided, as was the debate in the Synod, by our prayerful determination to know what is God's will for the Church at this point, and have been sustained by the collegial bonds among the members of the House which are one of God's gifts of grace to us. We have been informed by the views which many people have put to us in the period between the vote in Synod and our meeting.

4. We all recognise that the vote of the General Synod must be seen as part of a wider process within the Church of England, within the Anglican Communion and within the universal Church in which the question of women's ordination to the priesthood is being tested. We have been greatly helped in our own deliberations by the work, for example, of the Lambeth Conference of 1988 and the two reports of the Archbishop of Canterbury's Commission on Communion and on Women in the Episcopate. The Synod's decision expresses the mind of the majority of the Church of England insofar as this can be ascertained, and (if it is confirmed by Parliament) will determine our canonical position as a Church in which women may be ordained to the priesthood. We recognise, however, that there are those who doubt the theological and/or ecclesiological basis of the decision, and we accept that these are views which will continue to be held within the Church of England, and that those who hold them remain valued and loyal members of the Anglican family. At the same time as we affirm that differing views about the ordination of women to the priesthood can continue to be held with integrity within the Church of England, we encourage a willingness on the part of all to listen with respect to the

views of those from whom they differ, and to afford a recognition of the value and integrity of each other's position within the Church.

5. We believe that the Anglican ethos and tradition which has been developed under God through our experience and history gives us particular resources for living through our present disagreements and uncertainties and doing so together. This ethos, tradition and communion include commitment to Biblical authority, Trinitarian worship, respect for traditional doctrinal formulations, agreement about the need for an ordered and ordering ministry, and the practice of mutual responsibility and fellowship of a particularly open kind. Although we have differing interpretations, views and practices we maintain a shared commitment to belong together and to serve God together.

6. It is this developed practice and experience which gives us the basis for facing the reality of living with our differing convictions and with the necessary difficulties of carrying out any particular arrangements which we work out together in order to stay together. It is no shame to agree both to differ and to live, sometimes fearfully, together in the service of God. Rather it is a way of responding to God's leading into truth, in ways which are not yet clearly perceived by any of us.

7. It is with these convictions that we remain determined that:
   - the process of selection for ordination should remain fair, open and welcoming to different shades of opinion on this question and should not discriminate between candidates on the ground of their views about the ordination of women to the priesthood.
   - there should not be any such discrimination in preferment of priests to the episcopate or other senior positions in the church. We believe that the pastoral arrangements which we go on to outline can help to ensure the continued presence within posts of this nature of those with objections to the ordination of women to the priesthood as well as of those who welcome the decision of the Synod.

8. In what follows we express our firm intention to maintain the ecclesial integrity of the Church, including the historic threefold ministry of bishops, priests and deacons, while acknowledging the need to accommodate a diversity of convictions, particularly in matters relating to the Church's sacramental life. We are committed to maintaining the over-all unity of the Church, including the unity of each diocese under the jurisdiction of the diocesan bishop. We believe that such unity is essential to the overall effectiveness of the Church's mission to bring the Gospel of Christ to all people.

9. We intend to ensure that provision continues to be made by the diocesan bishop for the care and oversight of everyone in his diocese. We commit ourselves to uphold resolution 72 of the 1988 Lambeth Conference on episcopal responsibilities and diocesan boundaries[1]. Our proposals also reflect the shared intention we stated at our meeting in June 1992 to seek:

> "– to remain in communion with one another as Bishops of one Church;
> – to maintain the unity and integrity of the Church of England;
> – to uphold lawful authority within the Church of England;
> – to continue to provide episcopal oversight and pastoral care for all members of the Church."

10. Those of us who have objections to the ordination of women to the priesthood acknowledge that once the General Synod has promulged Canon C4B and Amending Canon No. 13 it will be possible for women lawfully to be ordained as priests in the Church of England. Those of us who favour the ordination of women to the priesthood acknowledge that in spite of this, there remain those who have theological and/or ecclesiological objections to such a step. Whatever his view on the ordination of women to the priesthood, each diocesan bishop will continue to accept full responsibility for

the episcopal oversight and pastoral care of all in his charge, whatever their view on this issue. Where necessary he will extend this care in appropriate ways.

11. In making such provision we do not and we cannot accept the theological reasoning behind the view that in some way those bishops and priests who participate in the ordination of women to the priesthood, thereby invalidate their sacramental ministry. Further we envisage that any bishop appointed to assist us in making any extended sacramental provision will remain in full communion with all members of the House of Bishops irrespective of whether or not such members have ordained women priests.

12. We have for some time been considering the practical implications of these principles and many of us are already taking steps towards making appropriate arrangements within our own diocese. These arrangements may entail:

   – a diocesan bishop not himself ordaining women while permitting his suffragans or assistants to do so;
   – a diocesan bishop authorising a suffragan or assistant bishop from within the diocese to minister on his behalf to clergy and parishes whose views on this issue differ from his own.
   – a diocesan bishop, with the approval of the Primate of the Province concerned, making such arrangements with a bishop (whether diocesan, suffragan or assistant) from a neighbouring diocese.

We shall be discussing with colleagues on a regional basis how best such arrangements could be made and the procedures which will be necessary to underpin them, for example in respect of mutual consultation over senior appointments.

13. To facilitate such arrangements we envisage the appointment of not more than three bishops (two in the Province of Canterbury and one in York) to act as Provincial Visitors

with specific responsibility to assist the diocesan bishop in the provision of appropriate ministry. These might be the holders of existing suffragan sees but it might also be necessary to create new posts for this purpose and this might involve synodical action. Among the tasks of a Provincial Visitor would be:

–    to work with the diocesan bishop in enabling extended pastoral care and sacramental ministry to be provided as might be apropriate;
–    to act as spokesman and adviser for those who remain opposed to the ordination of women to the priesthood and to assist the archbishops in monitoring the arrangements made for them.

14. Over the coming months we intend to discuss with our clergy and people precisely what arrangements on these lines are necessary in each diocese and how they would operate. We shall also be encouraging discussions at deanery level about how a proper diversity of pastoral ministry can be within reach of all our people. We are aware that differences of opinion between lay people are to be found, not only between parishes, but also within them. A willingness to cooperate within deaneries will therefore be necessary if different needs are to be met, and this will require generosity and Christian courtesy among clergy and laity alike.

15. At our meeting in June we will seek in the light of discussion in dioceses and in the church at large to give more detailed guidance on the arrangements which will operate. We will also consider again, with a view to finalising, the draft Code of Practice on the legislation which was included in GS Misc 336.

16. The arrangements which we have outlined do not detract from the safeguards in clauses 2, 3 and 4 of the Priests (Ordination of Women) Measure. They involve a willingness on the part of of all to act sensitively and flexibly, with

full recognition of the integrity of those who hold differing views on the ordination of women to the priesthood. We believe that they will ensure the maximum degree of communion between those of differing views while allowing the space which is necessary if this diversity is to be maintained within a framework of legitimate order. There are many aspects of communion: it is not an all-or-nothing state of relationship. Even where full sacramental communion may be restricted, members of the Church of England will continue to participate in the common goods of a shared baptism, shared faith, shared history, shared mission, and shared material resources and responsibilities. If different traditions are to continue alongside one another in fruitful interchange, it is essential that those who belong to them should play their full part at parish, deanery, diocesan and national level as far as conscience allows.

17. Rejoicing that our common life is life in the Spirit, we call on all members of the Church to continue in prayer, to join in positive discussions of how these proposals should be implemented in the months ahead, and to spare no effort to make fast with bonds of peace the unity which the Spirit gives.

1. The resolution stated–
   "This Conference:

   1 Reaffirms its unity in the historical position of respect of diocesan boundaries and the authority of bishops within these boundaries; and in light of the above.
   2 Affirms that it is deemed inappropriate behaviour for any bishop or priest of this Communion to exercise episcopal or pastoral ministry within another diocese without first obtaining the permission and invitation of the ecclesial authority thereof."

# Notes on Contributors

**Peter Newman Brooks**, University Lecturer in Divinity (Ecclesiastical History) and Fellow of Robinson College, Cambridge, has published a number of sixteenth-century studies, among them *Thomas Cranmer's Doctrine of the Eucharist* (2nd edition, Macmillan, 1992), and the popular documented life of Henry VIII's Archbishop, *Cranmer in Context* (Lutterworth, 1989).

**Hugh Craig** is a Chartered Mechanical Engineer, educated at Highgate School and Bristol University, and now retired as Technical Director of an engineering company. A Reader since 1946, he has been a member of the House of Laity of the Church Assembly and General Synod continuously since 1950, representing the laity of six dioceses. He has served as an elected member of the Standing Committee from 1965 to 1980 and since 1985: and as an elected Church Commissioner from 1987-1993.

**G. R. Evans** is a Lecturer in History in the University of Cambridge and member of the Faith and Order Advisory Group of the Church of England's General Synod. She is author of *Authority in the Church: a challenge for Anglicans* (Canterbury Press, 1990), *Problems of Authority in the Reformation Debates* (Cambridge University Press, 1992), and editor of *Christian Authority: Essays in Honour of Henry Chadwick* (ed.), (Oxford, 1988).

**Christine Hall** is Vice-Principal of Chichester Theological College and formerly parish deacon of St. George's Parish, Bickley, in the Diocese of Rochester. She read theology at King's College, London, and has taught Christian doctrine in which she has an M. Phil. She also serves on the Lambeth Diploma Committee. Her work with the British Council, where she was involved in the Middle East and North Africa, has given her wide experience and interest in development issues. She has written in particular on the Romanian Orthodox Church and has translated a number of Romanian theological and literary works into English. She is author of the chapter on the Orthodox Church in *Confession and Absolution* (SPCK, 1990), and editor of *The Deacon's Ministry* (Gracewing, 1991).

**Robert Hannaford**, a priest of the Church of England, is a Senior Lecturer in the Department of Religious Studies at Christ Church College, Canterbury, and was formerly Tutor in Christian Doctrine at St. Stephen's House and a member of the Faculty of Theology in the University of Oxford.

**The Rt Reverend Edward Knapp-Fisher** was educated at the King's School, Worcester, Trinity College, Oxford and Wells Theological College, Subsequently he was Chaplain (and later Principal) of Cuddesdon Theological College, Chaplain of St John's College, Cambridge, and from 1960-75 Bishop of Pretoria. In 1975 he was appointed to a Canonry at Westminster Abbey. Since his retirement in 1987 he has lived in Chichester where he is an honorary Assistant Bishop and Custos of St Mary's Hospital.

**Mrs Margaret Laird**, the Third Church Estates Commissioner was formerly Head of the Religious Studies Department at the Dame Alice Harpur School, Bedford. She has been a member of the General Synod since 1980.

**Lynne Leeder** read theology and law at Girton College, Cambridge. During that period she studied canon law with E. Garth Moore and completed a thesis on the seal of the confessional. A member of Lincoln's Inn, she practised at the Chancery Bar before joining the government legal service. Whilst working for the government she was seconded to the Overseas Development Administration and acted as an advisor to the government of Sierra Leone. She was a contributor to *The Deacon's Ministry* (Gracewing, 1991).

**The Reverend John Rees** is a practising Solicitor and Deputy Registrar of the Diocese of Oxford. He was ordained in 1979 and worked as a parish priest in Leeds and as a Theological College lecturer in Sierra Leone before returning to legal practice with a firm that specialises in ecclesiastical law. He is a Non-Stipendary Minister and assists with training of non-stipendary clergy for the Diocese of Oxford.

**Geoffrey Rowell** was born and brought up in Hampshire. He took a First in Theology at Corpus Christi College, Cambridge, in 1964, and was ordained in 1968 after completing his doctorate at Cambridge and training for the ministry at Cuddesdon. From 1968-72 he served as Assistant Chaplain at New College, Oxford, and since 1972 has been Fellow, Chaplain, and Tutor in Theology at Keble College, Oxford, and a University Lecturer since 1977. He served on the Liturgical Commission from 1981-1991, and since 1991 has been a member of the Doctrine Commission. A Canon of Chichester Cathedral since 1981, he has considerable ecumenical experience with the Orthodox churches and is currently a member of the Anglican- Oriental Orthodox International Forum. He has written widely on Anglican Church history, and on liturgical subjects. Among his publications are: *Hell and the Victorians, The Vision Glorious: themes and personalities of the Catholic revival in Anglicanism*; and as editor, *Tradition Renewed*, and *The English Religious Tradition and the Genius of Anglicanism*.

**The Reverend David Samuel** was formerly Director of the Church Society and is now Minister of St Mary's Episcopal Chapel, Reading.

**Michael Watts**, formerly Precentor of Christ Church, Oxford, is Rector of Sulhamstead Abbots with Sulhamstead Bannister and Ufton Nervet in the Diocese of Oxford. He is also Secretary of the Society for the Maintenance of the Faith and Warden of the Society of the Precious Blood, Burnham Abbey, Buckinghamshire.

**Father Edward Yarnold** is a Jesuit Priest at Campion Hall, Oxford, and a Research Lecturer in Theology in the University of Oxford. He was a member of ARCIC from its inception in 1970 to 1991. He was awarded the Cross of the Order of St Augustine by Archbishop Robert Runcie in 1981.

# Index

Abbot, Dean Eric 9
*Act of Supremacy* 14
*Act of Uniformity* 14; 99
— failure to repeal section 10; 99
  (see also *Church of England
  (Miscellaneous Provisions)
  Measure* (1991) )
Additional Curates Society 11; 36
Adie, Bishop Michael E 24
*All One in Christ* (1980
  Lutheran-Catholic Statement)
  25
Alternative Episcopal Oversight
  131ff; 145; 152
  see also 'Manchester
  Statement, The')
Anglican Consultative Council
  (ACC) 44
*Anglicanism: The Thought and
  Practice of the Church of
  England ...* 56
*Apostles Creed* 22
*Apostolic Curae* (1896) 26; 64
*Apostolic Ministry, The* (1946) 66
ARCIC 24
— ARCIC I 26
— ARCIC II 75

— Roman Catholic response 54
*Archbishops Commission on
  Doctrine* (1938) 59; 60; 88ff
Association for Apostolic
  Ministry 38
*Athanasian Creed* 22
*Athens Statement* (1978) 25f; 27
Augustine St, of Hippo 82
— attitude to the Donatists 82
Authority 30ff-; 88ff
— Church's authority in relation
  to Scripture 115
— in local churches 113
Avis, Paul 66
— *Anglicanism and the Christian
  Church* 55
— *Ecumenical Theology* 54

Bavin, Bishop Timothy 45
Bede, Venerable 7; 8
Bishops 142ff
— Anglican doctrine contrasted
  with reformed 133
— appointment of 105n
— February 1987 report (on
  appointments) 148
— oath of allegiance to 150